NEWS *at* TEN

NEWS *at* TEN

a celebration of 32 years of television news

David Stanley

Introduction by Trevor McDonald

For Linda
from
Trevor McDonald
best wishes

B⊞XTREE

Acknowledgements

ITN would like to thank all those who
helped to compile this book.

More importantly, thanks are due to anyone who,
in however small a way, has made *News at Ten* the
most successful news programme in Britain. The
accolades for the programme itself, its newscasters,
reporters and camera team depend on the
teamwork and professionalism of all its staff.

A special 'thank you' must go to *News at Ten*
viewers – the people for whom the programmes
are made – for their loyalty through the years.

MACMILLAN

First published in 1999 by Boxtree, an imprint of Macmillan Publishers Ltd,
25 Eccleston Place, London SW1W 9NF and Basingstoke.

Associated companies throughout the world.

ISBN 0 7522 1776 3

Text © Independent Television News Ltd, 1999

The right of Trevor McDonald to be identified as the author of the
introduction has been asserted by him in accordance with the
Copyright, Designs and Patents Act 1988.

9 8 7 6 5 4 3 2 1

A CIP catalogue record for this book is available from the British
Library.

Photographs © Independent Television News Ltd, 1999 except page
97, © Illustrated London News and pages 110 and 111, © Carlton
Television

Cover design by Simon Atyeo
Book design by Dan Newman

Research and interviews by Judy Lustigman
Archive and picture research by Mike Chandler

Colour reproduction by Speedscan Ltd
Printed in Great Britain by Butler & Tanner Ltd, Frome and London

The ITN logo and 'News at Ten' are trade marks of Independent
Television News Ltd registered in the UK and/or other countries and
are used under licence.

ITN website: www.itn.co.uk

Contents

Introduction

Shortly before the start of the Gulf War in l991 I went to Baghdad to interview President Saddam Hussein. Iraq's invasion of Kuwait with its explicit threat to Western interests made it a time of international tension. The business of actually getting to President Saddam Hussein was fraught with more personal stress. Of course, the Iraqis had agreed in advance to the interview or I wouldn't have been there. However as I quickly discovered, a verbal agreement with the Iraqi Ministry of Information is one thing. Hanging around the Al Rashid Hotel waiting for that agreement to be translated into action, was quite another. In one of those annoyingly interminable periods waiting for something to happen, those interstices or 'interims' – likened by Shakespeare to 'a phantasma or a hideous dream', I took a call from the Iraqi Ministry of Information. It was crisp and businesslike and carried an unmistakable note of urgency. I was to make my way to the Ministry at once. Believing that my big moment had come, or was at least near, I wasted no time.

But by the time we reached the Ministry a mere thirty minutes or so later, whatever sense of urgency there was, had mysteriously evaporated. Instead of confirming the time and place for my interview as I'd hoped, the Director explained to me with an expression brimming with *bonhomie* and pleasure, that all his officers had been to British universities and were all fans of *News At Ten*. As one of the presenters of the programme, they wanted to meet me, to shake me by the hand, to have me sign their autograph books and to question me about the programme's history and about why it had been such a great success. Before I could decide whether to be furious that this was not the expected appointment with the President or quietly pleased that *News At Ten* was so famous even in far-away Baghdad on the eve of battle, I was whisked off to meet the programme's Iraqi admirers.

Had this been the only occasion when I had come up against the reputation of a programme for which I have always been so proud to work, I might have put it down to one of those oddities of a life in television. But *News At Ten*'s august reputation was no oddity. It had been devised, nurtured and shaped as the ITN flagship, at a time when television news was about to enter an age of real competition. At its inception in 1967 *News At Ten* made commercial television history in Britain, and right up to its final weeks it continued to be the trailblazer of all serious television news programmes.

Those of us who have worked on the programme have always been struck by the fact that the strongest criticisms directed at what we've done over the years, amounted frequently to nothing more than the belief that we might have fallen short of the lofty standards we ourselves had set. To have been a part of such a record and such a tradition has been to appreciate what it means to belong to an institution. In the largely transient world of television, there are few great institutions. Having travelled the world for *News At Ten* for some twenty years, I have always been aware wherever I went that I was part of one of the few.

Ten years or so ago in Uganda we managed to attract too much attention from plain-clothes security police for filming in the streets of the capital Kampala without the permission of the Ugandan Ministry of Information. I had misrepresented the seriousness of the offence until the Ugandan policemen, seething with rage, cornered us in one of the city squares. Brooking no contradiction, they instructed us to accompany them to a nearby prison. That sanction sounded much graver than our supposed crime, but the demeanour of the policemen suggested to me that it was more prudent to obey than not to. As we were marched up the street to the local lock-up, a Range Rover going quite quickly, swerved to one side, screeched to a stop and reversed until it reached a point level with our group. In a high state of anxiety the driver emerged shouting: 'Trevor McDonald, *News At Ten.*' 'ITN... *News At Ten, News At Ten,*' he kept saying, and then more directly to me, 'May I have your autograph?'

At no point did the man betray the slightest understanding or interest in our predicament, although, having got his wish, he did agree to make two telephone calls at my request – one to the British High Commission and a second to our producer, passing on the news of our arrest.

The story is not without some significance. *News At Ten*'s presenters were all journalists and ITN had pioneered the 'reporter package' and the involvement of its journalists in the events they were assigned to report. It was not intended to influence what we reported nor was it an attempt to create a personality cult among its people. It was rather a way of legitimizing a connection between an event and the person charged with the task of bringing it to our viewers. It gave the reporter a stake in what he or she

was doing. It gave the viewers a point of reference by which a story could be followed and assessed. In many instances it humanized the stories we told and frequently made them more accessible, without ever deviating from the accuracy, balance and fairness demanded of all reporting. It also helped the ITN branding in unexpected ways. It's almost impossible for example in our television age to talk about the Turkish invasion of Cyprus in 1974 without linking it to the way it was reported by *News At Ten*. The report gave the event a status, an identity and put it squarely in the catalogue of twentieth-century television history. Who among us can forget the pictures of Turkish paratroopers falling out of the skies over Cyprus, to be met by our cameras and by our reporter with the words: 'Michael Nicholson, ITN, welcome to Cyprus.' It was a television moment twenty years ahead of its time. Looking back at it even now, there is a distinct echo of one of the most quoted sayings of the Canadian media guru Marshall McLuhan. That day in Northern Cyprus the medium did indeed become the message.

With equal distinction ITN devoted a great deal of time and ingenuity to bringing man's journey to the last frontier – the challenge of the conquest of outer space – to our audience. Here was *News At Ten* at its innovative best. The story of the space race between the Russians and the Americans and the whole concept of men planting earthly footsteps on the surface of the moon and exploring the unknown regions of other planets captivated the world and *News At Ten* was determined to play its role. We devised new graphics, constructed our own lunar models, and engaged scientists and astronauts to expand our own frontiers of television news reporting. The coming of the space age had made history. We wanted to make that point, but the people responsible for running *News At Ten* were determined too that our viewers should enjoy and share in the fun and exhilaration of what we were doing. That was a new departure in television news and one which never ceased to inform the style of what *News At Ten* did. It is perhaps equally true to say that in the minds of our viewers no less, it set us apart from our competitors. *News At Ten* has tried never to be pompous and we have tried never to take ourselves too seriously nor to stand on ceremony.

The space race between the Russians and the Americans was a pale reflection of the more sombre political realities of the Cold War. Like news organizations around the world, *News At Ten* devoted a great deal of air time to reporting it. We followed the enlargement of the European Common Market as it was then called, and our cameras told the story of the Israeli invasion of Beirut and the human tragedies of the massacres and hostage-taking that ensued. In South Africa the authorities made a direct connection between the profile of our reports and the temper of political protests in their country. They tried to censor what we and other journalists were able to film and what we were able to say. It didn't work. They never succeeded in shutting out the world's media. In a very real sense apartheid became more discredited, more unjustifiable and more untenable precisely because television news reports, among others, enabled the outside world to see and hear what the system was really doing to the lives of millions of men, women and children caught in its web. We were not alone in exposing the system's inherent contradictions. We are proud though to have played our part.

A book like this is bound to be more of an impressionistic review of the highlights of what we've done, than a precise and structured history of a television news programme. That awaits another, more impartial voice. What is beyond question though is that in the course of the last ten years two great themes have emerged from the focus of much of our reporting. The first is the collapse of the old Soviet Union and the manifold consequences for Eastern Europe of the end of the Cold War. The second has been the gut-wrenching human tragedy of so many internecine battles and civil wars.

News At Ten reported with great interest the declining fortunes of the Soviet gerontocracy. I went to Moscow for the programme to hear Leonid Brezhnev try to explain to a Communist Party Congress why the Soviets had invaded Afghanistan and why the traditionally troubled Soviet economy had been made worse by the invasion. Even in the claustrophobic world of Soviet politics Brezhnev's explanation didn't wash. It triggered a sequence of events which would change the Soviet Union and the face of the old Soviet Empire in Eastern Europe for ever. Through the eyes and reports of correspondents in Moscow and in Eastern Europe, *News At Ten* watched the crumbling Soviet empire fall apart. And we were there when that most potent symbol of communist repression – the Berlin Wall – was pulled apart almost brick by brick by people driven by heady thoughts of freedom. We were of course captivated by the Gorbachev overtures to the West – the man Mrs Thatcher openly said she could do business with – and our reporters were there to chart for our viewers what appeared to be the emergence of the old Soviet Union from its cocoon of authoritarian demagoguery. Gorbachev enjoyed summits with Western leaders and we enjoyed reporting them on *News At Ten*. I shall never completely lose from my mind the image of Ronald Reagan being met by goose-stepping Soviet soldiers in the capital of what the American President had called 'the evil empire'. We were convinced the world was changing. Gorbachev's fall from grace was almost as rapid as his rise and today our Moscow correspondent reports the turmoil in Russia as an ailing President tries to stamp the will of his administration on what is an increasingly ungovernable Russia.

A continuing article of faith at ITN, almost throughout my years here, was that the death of Marshall Tito of Yugoslavia would have grave consequences for the Balkans and for countries beyond them. Those consequences proved an important feature of *News At Ten*'s life in the last ten years and they shaped in our own minds a clear view of what our role has been in television news and what it should continue to be. In reporting the chaotic and bloody fall-out from the fracturing of Yugoslavia we came upon atrocities as grotesque and as obscene as any our civilization has known in recent times. Very early on in the fighting in Bosnia one of our colleagues discovered camps where people were being starved into brutal submission. Our reports focused the minds of world leaders on what had been going on in the former Yugoslavia. We would never make the arrogant claim *News At Ten* had the power to make world leaders listen, but after our story about the camps, they did, and there began a concerted diplomatic effort to find a solution to the problems in the Balkans. In their finest moments that is what serious, responsible news programmes should aim to do. They should give us pause, make us reflect on the consequences of what has occurred. More than that they should speak for the persecuted and the dispossessed and they should try to make absolutely sure that the plight of all those who struggle to survive under the yoke of oppressive regimes, is never lost on the world. As I write, after another massacre in Kosovo , we hope that in all humility, we are continuing to do just that.

In recent years we have spent a great deal of time reporting the appalling bloodletting in Rwanda and famines in other parts of Africa like the Sudan. Our reports and those of countless journalists in every branch of the media, have helped to inform the rest of the world how people in these situations can be assisted to re-build their lives. That, in my personal view, is in the finest tradition of our journalistic craft.

It's been a privilege to be part of the history of *News At Ten*. This has been so, not only because of what we have succeeded in doing in our reports from Bosnia or Rwanda or Eastern Europe, but also because of the opportunity to rub shoulders with the finest and the most distinguished and to follow in the footsteps of many of the best known names in British journalism. And by that I think not only of all those great and famous names who've graced our screens, but those of my colleagues who as editors, producers, writers, directors and engineers have made ITN what it is today. As we salute the years of *News At Ten*, we at ITN are determined to ensure that the best of its traditions never die, but live on to shine anew, in the programmes that now find their place in the new schedule on ITV.

I am delighted to have been asked to write this introduction to a book which I believe captures the essence of some of what we've done over the years. I hope it will be enjoyed by everyone interested in the record of one of the institutions of the television world.

Trevor McDonald

1967

IT HAD BEEN a sunny summer's day in London. There had been eleven hours of sunshine – beating down on ITN's cramped rooftop studio on the eighth floor of Television House in Kingsway. Rehearsals had been going on all evening. By ten o'clock, the temperature inside was well over ninety degrees. Newscasters Alastair Burnet and Andrew Gardner had to sit surrounded by ice trays and electric fans to try to keep cool as the production assistant counted down to transmission. The now famous *News at Ten* theme tune played, then came the chimes of Big Ben: the bongs.

And so was born *News at Ten* – Britain's first half-hour television news. No British news programme had ever been longer than fifteen minutes. Until then, the main ITN news programme of the day had been at 8.50pm and lasted just under fifteen minutes. There was no lunchtime news but there was an early evening news at around 5.50pm. BBC news programmes were similarly short. ITN did make one half-hour documentary programme called *ITN Reports* but that was shown only once a week.

News at Ten began as a three-month trial. The scripts for that first night's programme are labelled *Half - hour News* rather than *News at Ten*, but it was with the latter title that it was to last almost thirty-two years.

The dawn of the satellite age meant more international news could be covered, creating a growing appetite for pictures from around the world.

The first transmission by satellite of television pictures had happened five years earlier when the Telstar satellite was launched. Satellites brought an immediacy to television news pictures from, principally, the United States. From the early 1960s British television viewers could see something that had occurred thousands of miles away, across the Atlantic, on the day it happened – or sometimes even live *as* it happened. That immediacy captured the viewers' imaginations. Satellite transmissions meant there was enough material to fill comfortably a half-hour news programme. So too did new electronic links with other European TV stations and with the newsrooms of the various ITV companies around the country.

The headlines on 3 July 1967 went like this:

Railway strike called off
More fighting on the Suez Canal
The Queen at Expo '67
Taylor in Wimbledon semi-final

Then Alastair Burnet appeared, reading the introduction to the first story.

'Good evening. The railway freight strike has been called off. The railwaymen's union decided this tonight at the conference at Aberdeen, where Richard Dixon reports.'

It wasn't the most interesting story of all time. Indeed, the day's news agenda was quite cruel to the

On patrol with British troops – the 1st Battalion Argyll and Sutherland Highlanders – in Aden in July, as Arabs fought against British rule. One hundred and twenty-eight years of colonialism ended in November.

News at Ten team. It was like many in the summer months – the time of year referred to by journalists as the 'silly season'.

Only a few weeks earlier there had been a wealth of interesting stories. Israel had attacked its Arab neighbours in what became known as the Six Day War. The Liberian tanker, the *Torrey Canyon*, had run aground near the Scilly Isles and begun spewing out thousands of gallons of oil. On a rather lighter note, Francis Chichester came sailing up the English Channel at the end of his single-handed round-the-world voyage. But the new production team had to

work with what they'd got. In one sense it made the programme easier because there were no late changes to the carefully rehearsed running order. That first night's programme wasn't without its teething troubles though. A map used in the story about Suez came up three times – but for all that, an important step had been taken.

Alastair summed up the aims and aspirations of the programme in his closing script after the final report:

'… which brings us to the end of this, the first *News at Ten*. Our aim is to bring you every weekday evening a half-hour news in depth, at a peak viewing hour, a new venture in British television. For television itself is now better equipped to cover the world's news than it was when the old, short news bulletin was devised. We know it means asking you to develop a new viewing habit at ten o'clock every evening; but we mean to make it worth your while. Goodnight.'

News at Ten of course didn't just appear out of nowhere. ITN – Independent Television News – had started in September 1955, when the first ITV companies began broadcasting, breaking the monopoly of the BBC. The companies decided that a separate television station should be set up to make the news. ITN pioneered the technique of using newscasters to introduce reports – the first was the four-minute-mile hero, Christopher Chataway. Until then, the BBC and cinema newsreels had used disembodied voices to talk over the moving pictures. Robin Day became ITN's next famous newscaster, and Barbara Mandell was the first woman to read the news on British television. Even in those early days, ITN had something of a tradition of not neglecting the lighter side of life – a tradition more recently exhibited in the 'And Finally' slot at the end of most editions of *News at Ten*. The ITN programmes of the mid sixties attracted large audiences but it took a long battle with the ITV

companies to persuade them of the merits of a half-hour programme.

Among the many pioneering techniques of that first *News at Ten* was the use of two newscasters to help create more variety in presentation. When it came to selecting who was going to present the programme, Andrew Gardner was an obvious choice. An established ITN face, he had authority yet a popular touch. But who was to partner him on that first night? Alastair Burnet had worked for ITN as political editor but left and in 1967 was editor of *The Economist* magazine. He was invited back to present *News at Ten* for those first experimental months.

The other member of the team was Reginald Bosanquet, whom everyone inside and outside *News at Ten* knew as Reggie. ITN's editor Geoffrey Cox did have reservations about turning one of his dashing

reporters into a newscaster. The two skills are by no means the same. Another problem was that from birth Reggie suffered from a slight paralysis down one side of his face. It occasionally reappeared when he was tired and it could make it seem as though he was slurring his words.

The fourth member of the team would be Leonard Parkin. He would combine presenting the early evening bulletins with *News at Ten*.

Another big change in presentation pioneered by *News at Ten* in those early programmes was initially thought to be a 'minor alteration' but it changed television news reporting out of all recognition.

Up to this point, film shot on location was first edited to a given length according to its pictorial value. A writer then prepared a script broadly based on the notes given to him or her by the reporter on the spot. That script was then read out by a voice in the studio. The new idea involved reversing this procedure so that the reporter recorded a commentary in the field. Now his or her voice would be heard over the film which was then edited to match it. Film editing booths were placed in the newsroom. From now on it would be the reporters who called the shots. The effect on the screen was electric. Viewers had a taste of being on the spot with the action rather than attending an illustrated lecture from a disembodied voice. The reporter was clearly placed in charge of his own report. While the technology and style of news reporting have changed considerably since that time, the principle is exactly the same today.

Part of the original *News at Ten* team in 1967 (opposite) and again at the programme's thirtieth anniversary in 1997 (below). Left to right in both pictures: director Diana Edwards-Jones, programme editor David Nicholas, newscasters Alastair Burnet and Andrew Gardner, and reporter George Ffitch.

The difficulties of finding enough interesting reports to fill that first programme highlighted another problem. Then, as now, *News at Ten* had to be a specific length. Everyone had got used to the fifteen-minute news. Getting the sums as well as the journalism right took a bit of practice.

Production staff had other problems to contend with. The newsroom was on the seventh floor of Television House, which was the home of Associated Rediffusion, the London ITV company. The studio and control room were on the floor above. A staircase took you from the newsroom to the control room but only via the studio. When the studio was locked, as it had to be during transmission, the only way to get between the newsroom and the control room was on an outdoor metal gantry. That was a ghastly experience for anyone with vertigo or at night in the dark, or in bad weather. And anyone walking along it during transmission could be heard in the studio – making a sound like a distant herd of elephants.

Alastair Burnet and Reginald Bosanquet presenting an early *News at Ten* during the three-month trial for the new half-hour programme.

On the second Tuesday the new *News at Ten* did get the break it had been waiting for and made the most of it. Ballet stars Rudolf Nureyev and Margot Fonteyn had been arrested in a hippy area of San Francisco by police after a drugs raid at a party they were attending. ABC television in America had film of the two stars being questioned in a nearby police station. The only way of getting it to London was to pay around £6,000 for a land-line transmission from San Francisco to New York and then a satellite across the Atlantic. That was very expensive but, with the long-term success of the programme at stake, it seemed a worthwhile investment. British viewers of the new programme were treated to something of a television feast. The scene was straight out of an American detective series. There was the crowded precinct office. There were the filing cabinets. There were the desk tops strewn with used coffee cups with a detective asking, 'How do you spell a name like Nureyev? Is it N like Nobody, U like United States…' It was human interest *par excellence*. It helped swing the critics and the viewers *News at Ten*'s way.

The all-important viewing figures for the first week of the new programme put all five editions of *News at Ten* in the top twenty – Monday night's programme was number five in the chart and Thursday's was number eight. Then, often as now, *Coronation Street* was the most popular programme of the week.

With the establishment of ITN, there had been concerns about a possible conflict of interest between a commercial television network, paid for with advertisements, and an independent news company. These fears had long been allayed by ITN, its impartiality a matter of record. *News at Ten*,

Andrew Gardner

Andrew Gardner was born in Beaconsfield in Buckinghamshire in 1932 and educated in Wiltshire. After National Service in the RAF, he worked in Central Africa where, in 1957, he joined the Federal Broadcasting Corporation of Rhodesia and Nyasaland as a trainee reporter. He subsequently became a current affairs producer.

Returning to live in England in 1961, Andrew worked as a writer on African affairs and as a freelance broadcaster for the overseas service of the BBC. His first experience of television was as host of a BBC live lunchtime discussion programme called *Table Talk*.

In December 1961 Andrew joined ITN as a newscaster and reporter. He was also the anchorman for a wide range of special programmes which included the Cuban crisis, the assassination of President Kennedy, general elections and budgets. He has been an ITV commentator for state occasions including the Queen's Silver Jubilee and royal weddings.

He and Alastair Burnet were the newscasters on the historic first night of *News at Ten* in 1967. Andrew continued as a presenter of the programme until he left ITN in 1977 to join Thames Television as anchorman for Thames News. He was co-host of the first ITV *Telethon* in 1986 and also anchored a number of special ITV network programmes. He retired in 1992.

however, did reopen the debate somewhat – even among the company's own journalists – as it would be the first news programme to have advertisements in the middle. Some feared commercial concerns might compromise the programme's news values. But then, as now, *News at Ten* never let what was in the commercial break affect its decision-making.

Six weeks after the programme was launched, its success in the ratings guaranteed that the thirteen-week 'experiment' was now to be confirmed as a regular feature of the country's viewing. The commercial break in the middle of the programme was also judged to have been a success. That too would continue. It was later to become, and remain, one of the most expensive commercial breaks in British television.

However, the end of the experimental period did mean the end of Alastair Burnet's initial stint presenting *News at Ten*. He had of course agreed only to help launch the programme during the summer. The time had come for him to return full-time to his job as editor of the *Economist*. He agreed to carry on doing occasional work for ITN; Alastair would return

Colonel Odumegwu Ojukwu, who led the breakaway of Biafra from Nigeria, being interviewed by Sandy Gall in July as Nigerian Government troops advanced on Biafra's capital, Enugu.

Johnny Pearson, pictured here in 1992, the composer of 'Arabesque'. This was the *News at Ten* title music throughout the programme's thirty-two years.

to the programme in 1977 to become its on-screen journalistic figurehead in the late seventies and through the eighties. Leonard Parkin would fill in the gaps. The dominant partnership, though, would be that of Andrew and Reggie.

Andrew Gardner remembers it like this: 'For me the golden years of *News at Ten* were the first ten. We had a fantastic team. Reggie and I had a distinct and unique partnership. We called ourselves "The Morecambe and Wise" of current affairs. We were both very serious presenters, but we had a chemistry that worked extremely well. I was the straight man and he was the knockabout comedian. The viewers identified with us and the viewing figures reflected that.'

Much has changed on *News at Ten* since that first week. One thing that hasn't – well, not much anyway, is the title music. The tune is called 'Arabesque' and was written by Johnny Pearson, who went on to write many other television theme tunes. The decision to use it was taken only at the last minute and after the first week it was nearly dropped. Viewers were complaining it was too harsh. A composer from Disney was called in during that first week to write a new theme tune. But an ITN sound mixer called

Alfie Wilson wanted to stick with the old tune. He took the original recording of 'Arabesque' to a nearby music studio and got it re-mixed – smoothing out some of the strident tones of the original. By the second Monday of *News at Ten* there was still no decision on which piece of music to use. Just before the programme started, editor Geoffrey Cox said, 'Let's go with what we've got for the time being.' Alfie played his re-mixed version on air and that's the one that was played five nights a week until a new arrangement of 'Arabesque' was created for the revamp of 1992.

The bongs came about by something of a happy accident. During the weeks of rehearsal, there was a debate about how many chimes of Big Ben should be heard. Director Diana Edwards-Jones was experimenting with a first edit of the new titles and a recording of the chimes. By coincidence, Andrew was in the studio practising how he might read the introduction, which was going to go something like, 'Good evening. Here is the news. The *Torrey Canyon* is bombed …' and so on. Because of a misunderstanding with the sound mixer, Andrew's words were brought up over the chimes. Diana noticed that the gap between the chimes almost fitted Andrew's words, so she got him to shorten them slightly. The rest is television history.

Beyond the studio, out in the field, the often dangerous work of reporters and their crews continued apace. In September an ITN crew had a narrow escape when a bomb was placed inside their camera equipment on board a Saudi Airlines plane in Yemen. Fortunately it didn't go off. The crew – cameraman Chris Faulds, sound recordist Barry Martin and reporter Richard Lindley – were returning to Jeddah from Najran when the steward on the Dakota plane noticed a strange smell coming from one of the camera boxes. When they opened the box there were eight sticks of explosives, crudely taped together. Detonators had been attached to each stick with slow-burning fuses but had failed to set off the main charge. It wasn't clear who placed the bomb among the ITN gear, or whether the idea behind it had been to kill the ITN crew or to blow up the plane in flight. It could have been someone who wanted to destroy the ITN film of Egyptian military activity in Yemen. The pilot somehow managed to land the plane on a desert airstrip but the danger for the ITN men wasn't over. They had to carry the box off the plane and away from the landing zone.

Back in the *News at Ten* studio Reggie found himself in a little local difficulty during an early live studio interview. His interviewee was Lee Kuan Yew, the Prime Minister of Singapore. In those days there was a special interview area but Reggie had forgotten to move from his newscaster position. As a result he had to conduct the interview at the top of his voice from one side of the studio to the other. The Prime Minister didn't seem to notice anything was wrong … at least he didn't say so if he did.

Which only goes to prove that the news is live and anything can go wrong – but fortunately rarely does.

And Finally...

A London GP, Dr Trevor Weston, told a British Medical Association conference in Bristol that people whose surname began with letters from S to Z were twice as likely to get ulcers; three times as likely to suffer a heart attack; and will live – on average – twelve years less than the rest of the population.

Dr Weston called for more research to be made in what he called 'the Alphabetic Neurosis' to help the unfortunate members of the S to Z club.

1968

THE RUSSIAN INVASION of Czechoslovakia – the crushing of the 'Prague Spring' of protest against Soviet oppression – brought a classic David and Goliath battle on to British television screens. One piece of film shown on *News at Ten*, which graphically illustrated what was going on there, arrived at ITN after being smuggled out of the country in dramatic style. The film was taken by Czech cameramen, two of whom were wounded. One of them dropped the film – wrapped in brown paper – into a tourist's car near the border with Austria. Inside the parcel was a request that the film be shown throughout the world. The shaky, but heartrending, pictures showed an elderly woman screaming defiance at the passing Russian tanks, then a Czech flag dipped

Soviet tanks rolling into Czechoslovakia to crush the 'Prague Spring' of rebellion against rule from Moscow.

Michael Nicholson talking to a bemused and frightened Biafran prisoner. Moments later the man was shot dead in front of ITN's cameras.

in the blood of the first victim of a Russian bullet and Czech bodies lying under their country's flag in an alley.

Even more disturbing pictures brought home the horror of the Biafran war, which had started the previous year. An ITN crew came across an officer in the Nigerian Army as he was deciding what punishment to exact on a young Biafran man, whose hands were tied behind his back. As the ITN camera rolled, it looked like the Biafran wasn't going to be harmed, but then the officer shot dead the terrified

***News at Ten*'s main presenters of the late 1960s (opposite). Andrew Gardner seated left, Leonard Parkin standing, and Reginald Bosanquet, right.**

Peter Sissons at an aid station after being wounded during an ambush. A *Time-Life* reporter was killed in the same incident.

and confused man. An edited version of those events – though horrific to say the least – was shown on *News at Ten*. It was a decision that was later praised as responsible and courageous.

It was while he was reporting the Biafran war in October that Peter Sissons's career as an ITN foreign correspondent came to an end, after a terrifying attack in which he almost died. Peter and his cameraman Cyril Page had accepted an offer from the Nigerian armed forces to visit the front line. When they arrived at a roadblock, they got out of the bus they were travelling in and – with their army escort – started to walk. Suddenly they were caught up in the middle of a large ambush. Peter said there was a lull in the gunfire. He put his head out and heard someone loading a magazine into a rifle. 'I dived back into the hole I'd been hiding in, head first. My legs were in the air and one bullet went through both of them,' he said. He was shot by a Biafran soldier from about twenty feet away. Peter felt he didn't have long to live.

When Cyril found Peter, he was lying on the ground covered in mud and blood. Cyril slit open Peter's trousers and saw the holes in his legs – one was three or four inches across. Remembering his Boy Scout

training, Cyril tore up his shirt and made tourniquets to try to stop the blood flow. Peter was carried by his crew for half a mile on a makeshift stretcher – a plank of wood torn from the roof of a nearby building. A little later they found a pram so they lifted the plank, with Peter on it, on to the pram and pushed him until they came across a jeep that could take him to a ramshackle hospital – what Peter later called 'a pile of coffins with a man with a syringe'. There was no doctor there so they then had to drive sixty miles to the nearest proper hospital. They did their best to treat him there but said he needed to go to the main hospital in Lagos. The only way to get there was by plane. But when they got to the airport, there were no planes. In stifling heat they had to wait two days for a military aircraft. Even then it had to land on the road because the runway had been blown up. In the meantime ITN flew out an RAF surgeon to look after Peter and bring him home. When they finally arrived back at Heathrow there were words of thanks from ITN for the surgeon. 'Don't thank me,' he said. 'I've learned more about life from Cyril Page in the last two weeks than in all my twenty-one years in the RAF.'

Peter continued to need treatment for a year and the wounds to his legs left him with a slight limp. It also meant he could never work in war zones again. After resuming a less hazardous reporting career he went on to become the presenter of ITN's *News at One*, and ITN's *Channel Four News* before joining the BBC's *Nine O'Clock News* and *Question Time*.

There is a little postscript to the story, which involves the surgeon who treated Peter. Not long after Peter returned, Cyril's son – a cameraman with the ITV company Westward Television – was hurt in a fall from a television crane. He suffered broken ribs and was rushed to Taunton hospital. The doctor treating him said, 'That's strange. I've just come back from Lagos with another television cameraman called Page who works for ITN and brought out a badly injured reporter. I don't suppose you are by any chance related?'

News at Ten had been going for more than six months before it was decided to stamp the programme's identity on to every report with what is called a 'signoff'. That is when the reporter rounds off his or her report with their name, the name of the programme, and their location. The question was: when would be a good night to start doing it? The answer had to be when there were lots of reports expected from far flung, exotic-sounding locations. So we would hear, 'On Highway 19, South Vietnam', 'On the Aden-Yemeni border', 'On the civil rights march in Alabama', and 'At the manned Space Centre, Houston, Texas'. As fate would have it, a late story broke rather closer to home and went to the top of the programme. The first signoff the viewers heard that night was 'Richard Dixon, *News at Ten*, at the Ford works in Dagenham'.

The first anniversary of *News at Ten* gave television critics – many of whom initially took some converting – a chance to salute its achievements. One said it was 'artfully presented'. More importantly the viewers liked it too. In its anniversary week, *News at Ten* occupied three of the top four positions in the television charts. The programme on 1 July was the most watched of the week – thanks partly to an interview with the lone round-the-world yachtsman, Alec Rose.

The first firing of a Polaris missile by the British submarine HMS *Resolution*, filmed by ITN in February.

Sandy Gall reporting on the battle for Hue.

Within ITN itself, its editor Geoffrey Cox left to join Yorkshire Television. The new man was Nigel Ryan, promoted from within ITN, who announced his main priority would be strengthening and enhancing *News at Ten*.

By now the double act of Gardner and Bosanquet was well established and not just on the screen. During supper breaks they could occasionally be seen relaxing together – playing a game that involved bowling a rubber ashtray, shaped like a tyre and advertising a tyre company, down the long corridor on the seventh floor. The idea was to get it from one end to the other without it hitting the walls. Andrew recalled later that on one occasion he had just bowled a corker when the editor's door opened and

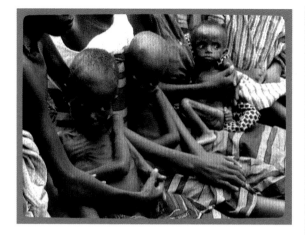

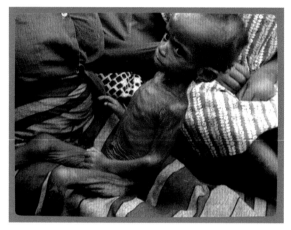

The haunting images of starving children in reports by ITN's Peter Snow brought home to *News at Ten* viewers the suffering caused by the fighting in Biafra.

when out of the corner of his eye he noticed a small Tunisian boy wearing a fez trudging through the sand towards them. He was the hotel errand boy and was carrying a telegram which turned out to be from Reggie. It read 'NIGEL EDITOR. YOU TEA-LADY.'

And Finally...

When people talk about air hostesses the picture usually conjured up is of that calm, reassuring person moving confidently along the aisle. When ITN reporter Robert Southgate went to Wycombe Air Park, Buckinghamshire, the last thing he expected was to see seven BEA stewardesses taking turns riding on the *outside* of an aircraft. The plucky group were practising for a charity air show to be held at Denham on 25 May. Robert interviewed one of them, Patricia Garner, on what it felt like ...

'Well,' she said, 'it's different, I'll say that, from the inside.'

'Was it exhilarating?' Robert asked.

'Yes,' Patricia replied, 'except that it's ruined every bit of my eye make-up.'

Asked if she would do it again, she answered, 'Yes, I would. Every time. I'd like to take it up as a hobby!'

he walked out. The ashtray shot between his legs at a rate of knots. When Andrew looked round for moral support from Reggie, he was nowhere to be seen. Andrew recalls one other story about Reggie that year which relates to the news of Geoffrey Cox's departure. When he left, the whole newsroom was eager to know who his successor was. Andrew had gone on his first ever winter holiday, to Tunisia. Before leaving, Andrew had begged Reggie to tell him who got the job the moment it was known. Andrew and his wife were lying in the sun one afternoon

Reginald Bosanquet

Reginald Bosanquet was a newscaster at the start of *News at Ten* in 1967 and his highly individual style of news-reading rapidly made him a celebrity. He was renowned for his lop-sided grin, slightly slurred speech, and unusual pronunciation of words such as 'rahlway'.

His exuberant lifestyle was often reported in the daily newspapers. In later years Reggie's toupee became an object of fascination among *News at Ten*'s viewers.

He was born in 1932, son of England cricketer B.J.T. Bosanquet, inventor of the 'googly'. Reggie was evacuated to Canada during the Second World War. On his return he studied at Winchester and New College, Oxford, where he read history.

In 1955, straight from university, he approached ITN for a job, saying he wanted to be a star. They said he could start as a tea-boy on £10 a week. He soon became a sub-editor and, in 1957, a reporter.

He was diplomatic correspondent for four years and in 1959 he was the anchor of ITN's *Dateline* programme, a post he held for eight years. His style of newscasting was less formal than the approach at the BBC. He once said that he 'tried to think myself into people's drawing rooms, rather than addressing the nation'.

Reggie left ITN in 1979, and died in 1984 at the age of fifty-one.

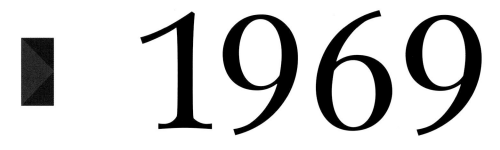

I T WAS A YEAR that saw two big changes – for those who worked at ITN and for those who watched. After fourteen years based at Television House in Kingsway in central London, ITN moved and with good reason. By now, just over 300 people worked for the organization. The new headquarters were in the West End – between Oxford Circus and the then Post Office Tower – in Wells Street. It was to be the most modern television news centre in the world, with two studios instead of just one. At first, the *News at Ten* set looked rather small in its spacious new studio. The other main reason for the move was the need for ITN to make *News at Ten* and its other programmes in colour, as the biggest revolution in television began. Staff went to lectures at the North London Polytechnic to learn how making colour programmes would be different from those in black and white. The lectures didn't really interfere with making programmes, because in those days the first ITN news of the day was at 5.50pm.

The pub next door to the new ITN House – The Green Man – soon became the venue for *News at Ten*'s own 'Match of the Day'. On days that Andrew Gardner and Reggie Bosanquet were presenting the programme together, they could sometimes be found playing bar billiards in The Green Man during the supper break that preceded the programme.

That friendship and mischief-making – on Reggie's part anyway – was in evidence the night the Queen came to ITN headquarters to officially open the new building. Andrew and Reggie were sitting opposite one another in the newsroom when the Queen and her entourage approached. Andrew was just about to start writing the 'bongs' on a piece of paper in his typewriter. Suddenly, as the Queen approached,

ITN's new headquarters in Wells Street in the West End of London – its home for the next twenty-one years.

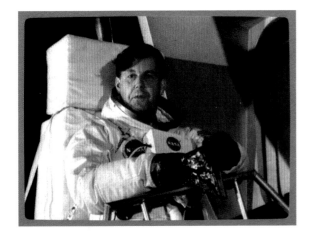

ITN science editor Peter Fairley demonstrating a space suit in the run up to the lunar landing in July.

Reggie jumped round the desk and typed a headline of his own on Andrew's typewriter. Then he stood back as the Queen moved towards the desk. The programme editor, who could see something had been written on the paper in the typewriter, said to Andrew, 'I'm sure Her Majesty would be interested to see how you are getting on with this evening's headlines.' Andrew felt himself start to sweat, tried to give an off-putting stare and said, 'Well, I don't think so – they are not really ready yet.' Andrew then tried to distract the royal party with a discussion on the lead stories. When the Queen moved away, Andrew tore the page from his typewriter. In capital letters at the top, Reggie had typed: 'ONE OLD QUEEN MEETS ANOTHER'.

Many who worked at ITN in 1969 believe they lived through the greatest news story of all time – the Apollo missions and man's first step on the moon. As ITN's deputy editor at the time, David Nicholas, remembered it, it was 'like being a correspondent with a notebook and camera as Christopher Columbus first stepped ashore in the New World'.

Early ITN space programmes had used Frank Sinatra's 'Fly Me to the Moon' as their theme tune. In May, special coverage of the Apollo 10 mission which approached within nine miles of the moon's surface won second place in the TV ratings. ITN had got something of an 'audience grabber' by adding to its reporting team Paul Haney – the official voice of NASA on previous missions.

The mission that was to land on the moon, Apollo 11, was due to touch down around 9.00pm London time one Sunday in July. Neil Armstrong was expected to make his historic walk on the moon's surface at 4.00am the following day. ITN's plan for covering it was to have a double-handed programme, starting at 6.00pm on the Sunday evening, where Alastair Burnet at ITN would present the happenings in space and David Frost at London Weekend Television would host an entertaining look at what it might be like to live on the moon. The programme would continue until the moonwalk had finished.

The ITV companies didn't much like the idea of that. They didn't mind a few newsflashes to keep viewers up to date but they didn't want to have to cancel normal Sunday night viewing. ITN thought one of its biggest opponents might be the head of ATV in the Midlands, Sir Lew Grade. While ITN executives were waiting to make their case to Sir Lew and other programme controllers, a sub-committee on religious broadcasting got in ahead, on apparently urgent business. Perhaps that affected Sir Lew's thinking. When he finally did see the ITN presentation he gave his approval for the programme

with the words, 'This is the biggest story since the birth of Jesus Christ.'

So it was 'all systems go' for the programme but there was a technical problem to overcome. Much of what the astronauts said was in code: for example, '1202, do you copy?' meant 'Shall we abort the mission?' The viewers had let it be known that they wanted to know what was being said but they didn't want presenters talking over the astronauts. At the time there was an early form of caption generator that could be programmed in advance so that every possible codeword the astronauts might use could be pre-programmed and then called up and put along the bottom of the screen when needed. The programming task fell to producer Frank Miles and it took several weeks. On the night of the landing, as the landing module disappeared behind the moon

David Nicholas, editor of *News at Ten* and ITN's space programmes, and science editor, Peter Fairley, meeting astronaut Neil Armstrong during his visit to ITN.

for the last time, starting its descent, the first caption appeared over the voices of the astronauts and Mission Control. Thanks to Frank's careful programming viewers could see, hear and understand what was going on all at the same time.

Unfortunately, halfway through the final descent the caption generator overheated and it stopped working. Foreseeing the problem, an engineer had brought with him a film can containing dry ice and a hair dryer to blow the cool air over the generator's overheated transistors. The final phase of descent was captioned again. It made breathtaking television as the astronauts' staccato conversations got

President Richard Nixon and Prime Minister Harold Wilson meeting for the first time during a brief visit by the American leader to London in February.

increasingly tense. As the legs of the 'Eagle' capsule touched the surface, Frank's assistant pushed the final button in the sequence stored on the caption generator which was still suffering slightly. The word that appeared on the screen was 'Ouchdown'.

News at Ten has always reported British feats of bravery and endurance. During 1969 a rower called John Fairfax was trying to make it single-handedly across the Atlantic, east to west. Michael Brunson was the reporter sent to America to watch him arrive. Unfortunately Michael and his crew got there rather too early – Mr Fairfax still had around three more weeks of rowing to go. So they had to undergo the hardship of lounging around a Florida hotel with nothing to do.

However, with consciences burning, they decided they must do something. They hit on the rather extravagant plan of hiring a sea plane so they could drop in on Fairfax, but to no avail. The sea plane couldn't land so Michael dropped messages and

boxes of cigars. Next, they hired a 140-foot yacht with a seven-man crew. They sailed alongside him and lifted him out of his rowing boat to do an interview with him. By now the bills for the assignment were running out of control. Even though the interview was filmed in black and white – and *News at Ten* was in colour by now – Michael's report occupied most of the second half of one programme, by way of justifying the expense. The monochrome nature of the interview wasn't the only thing about it that might have looked curious to viewers watching at home. During it, the light faded and the interviewee appeared to become a little the worse for wear. The yacht's crew had given Mr Fairfax a drink or two by way of welcome. Bear in mind he hadn't had any alcohol for three months. By the time the interview was done a rather 'drunken sailor' was eased back into his rowing boat. No surprise then, that it took him another two weeks finally to make dry land near Fort Lauderdale.

And Finally...

An American airline with an eye to future business started to advertise for the ultimate in get-away-from-it-all holidays. The moon.

The airline issued claim tickets for reservations on the first space flight to the moon. They also produced a brochure inviting the lucky tourists to try out such resort experiences as a 'moonhike round the craters'.

For those who preferred a less strenuous way of sightseeing you could leave your luxury lunar hotel by renting a moon car.

The applications could be sent to the California offices of the airline or, a little later they hoped, to their new premises. In Copernicus Crater.

1970

A HIJACK DRAMA played out in an airport in Jordan brought *News at Ten* one of its greatest coups. Terrorists belonging to the Popular Front for the Liberation of Palestine hijacked four planes on the same day. One hijack attempt was led by a woman called Leila Khaled and ended peacefully at Heathrow airport. She was arrested and imprisoned in London. Another ended in Cairo when a Pan-Am 747 was blown up just after the passengers and crew had been freed. The pilots of the other two planes were ordered to fly to Amman, the Jordanian capital. They landed at an old RAF airstrip north of Amman, at a place called Ga Khanna. In its RAF days it had been known as Dawson's Field after a former air vice-marshal.

There was soon to be another, much more alarming, British connection to the story. A BOAC VC-10 was hijacked in reprisal for Leila Khaled's arrest in London. There were more than a hundred passengers on board including thirty British schoolchildren. The British captain was ordered to fly to Amman too. Now there were three planes on the desert airstrip. Michael Nicholson was sent to cover the story with his Palestinian cameraman, Ghassan Dallal.

The terrorists were demanding the release of Leila Khaled and other PFLP members held in Israel, West Germany and Switzerland. They set a deadline of three days. If their demands weren't met by the relevant governments they would blow up all three planes with the passengers and crews still inside.

Fortunately, the hostages didn't know that. They had enough to worry about. The desert nights were freezing; the days scorching. There was little food or water and the lavatories were soon blocked. Both America and Britain began sending troops to the area as the tension increased. In reply the Palestinians placed explosives around the plane.

The day before the deadline was due to expire a scheduled Middle East Airlines jet flew into Amman's main airport. On board was David Phillips, ITN's senior producer. As he was arriving, news came through that a deal had been done. The passengers were to be freed. As Michael prepared his script for the story of their release his cameraman, Ghassan, said they had to go back to the airport. Michael wasn't sure why and Ghassan wouldn't say.

They arrived at the airfield as the final group of hostages was leaving one of the planes. Michael saw a group of terrorists jumping from the plane and running under the wings and nose. Then the Palestinians jumped into a jeep and sped away from the planes. Ghassan started his camera running. Almost immediately one plane exploded, then another and then the third. So how did Ghassan know what was going to happen? 'I am a Palestinian,' he said by way of reply. It turned out he was a member of the PFLP. He took the film to the PFLP's central committee saying it was for them to decide how it should be used. David Phillips managed to persuade them it would be most useful

The standoff over the three hijacked western airliners at Dawson's Field, near Amman in Jordan. ITN made television history when its cameraman captured the destruction of the planes by Palestinian terrorists.

to them on television screens around the world. When the film arrived back at ITN House it made, says newscaster Andrew Gardner, the most dramatic start to *News at Ten* that he could remember. He worked on a script with David Phillips. 'We scrapped the bongs that night,' says Andrew. 'It was a very exciting programme.'

The troubles in Northern Ireland provided their own particular difficulties in covering a story. To film at night, television cameras need lights. Those lights can give away the position of the camera team

which can cause both professional and personal problems. First of all, if someone knows they are being filmed they may behave or react differently or simply run off. Secondly, if someone involved in the conflict has a grievance with a camera team and wants to stop them filming or, worse, attack them, then lights act as a kind of neon sign, advertising where the camera is. By 1970 a new advance in night-time filming had been developed which helped solve the problem. It was an image intensifier – using a series of lenses that could be controlled electronically depending on just how little light there was.

Lights of a different sort were causing problems in the studios. They showed up too clearly the signs of ageing on the *News at Ten* newscasters.

Both Reggie Bosanquet and Sandy Gall began using proper television make-up one day in August. Reggie said at the time it was because his daughter said she thought he looked awful. He blamed his haggard appearance on having to work eleven days out of thirteen, instead of the usual four days in a row, to cover for his then ITN colleague Peter Snow who had been sent on assignment to the Middle East. No one else could stand in because it was holiday time and Leonard Parkin and Andrew Gardner were away. The public fascination about whether craggy-faced newscasters should or shouldn't wear make-up rumbled on in the newspapers for weeks.

In fact, in the early years of the programme there was no formal arrangement for make-up in the studio. Sometimes guests would come in expecting to be made up for the studio lights. On one visit, Barbara Castle, then a Labour government minister, came into the studio to be interviewed without wearing any make-up at all, expecting some professional attention. A production assistant had to run round the newsroom asking all the women to empty their handbags, assembling what she thought looked like a professional make-up set and then applying it to Mrs Castle's face. She was apparently perfectly happy with the result.

In 1970 a newly trained director, Nigel Warrack, was given his first programme to do. It was the culmination of months of training. The rehearsal went according to plan and there were still a couple of minutes to go before transmission. Nigel looked around and saw, standing behind him, two senior bosses. Nigel thought, 'How nice. They've taken the trouble to come down and wish me luck.' As the clock counted down towards transmission the production assistant said, 'Two minutes to on air.' At

that point one of the bosses, David Nicholas, then deputy editor, leaned over and whispered in Nigel's ear, 'Don't panic, but we've just been told there's a bomb scare in Studio 1. Do you think you can move and put the programme out from Studio 2?'

Nigel says his memories of those next two minutes are rather blurred as the team galloped down the corridor from one studio to the other, carrying scripts, stopwatches and clipboards. What he does remember is trying to push through dozens of people heading in the opposite direction as they evacuated the building. He and his team somehow scrambled on air with two cameras instead of the normal four. Nigel remembers thinking when it was all over that if he could direct that he could direct anything. He adds modestly, 'I was wrong, of course.'

And Finally...

Kent pet shop owner, Roy Tutt, claimed to have created a new breed called the 'puppy-cat'. He achieved this remarkable feat, he said, by crossing a female black cat with a male Scots Terrier. The animal was said to have the face of a puppy but a cat-like tail and claws.

Sandy Gall, CBE

Sandy Gall was born in Penang, in 1927, the son of a Scottish rubber planter. After graduating from Aberdeen University he worked for a short time on the *Aberdeen Press and Journal* and then moved to Reuters in 1953.

Sandy joined ITN in 1963 as a 'trouble-shooter'. From 1970 he combined a career as *News at Ten* newscaster and award-winning ITN foreign correspondent. He was one of the programme's senior newscasters until January 1990.

He covered wars and revolutions around the world, perhaps most memorably from Vietnam, Uganda, the Gulf and Afghanistan.

He was one of the first correspondents in Vietnam in 1965 when the US marines went in, and reported the Tet Offensive in 1967 and 1968. He was in Saigon when Vietnam fell to the Communists in 1975 and stayed on until he was forcibly flown out by the Communist authorities.

It was in 1982, while co-presenting *News at Ten*, that he made his first three-month trip to Afghanistan, which he considered seriously underreported. He returned several times to make reports for *News at Ten* plus three documentary programmes. In 1983 he set up the charity Afghanistan Appeal.

Early in 1991, Sandy Gall went to Riyadh as part of the Media Response Teams reporting on the military preparations for the long predicted Gulf War. He went missing from Riyadh and reappeared as the first Western journalist to report live from Kuwait only a few hours after the start of the allied invasion.

Sandy has written several books including two volumes of memoirs: *Don't Worry About the Money Now* and *News from the Front*.

In February 1987 Sandy Gall was awarded the Lawrence of Arabia memorial medal by HRH the Prince of Wales for his reporting of Afghanistan. The following year he was made a CBE.

1971

PIONEERING TELEVISION NEWS camera-work often stems from technological advances and the skill and enthusiasm of individual cameramen and women. *News at Ten* viewers saw amazing live underwater pictures of the big shipwreck story of the year – the SS *Niki* – thanks to cameraman Slim Macdonnell. What they didn't know was that Slim – real name John and a keen diver himself – nearly didn't live to tell the tale. His air ran out and he had to make an emergency ascent. When he was finally hauled on deck he was unconscious.

ITN's other big underwater story of the year – though in rather lighter vein – was the hunt for the Loch Ness Monster. News editor Don Horobin was determined to find out once and for all whether there really was a monster lurking in the deep. That summer he personally led a ten-man team with several lightweight cameras. Their water-borne equipment consisted of a submarine normally used for recovering spent torpedoes which had grab gear and headlights, plus a chartered tug equipped with a sonar sensing device. For ten days they swept the loch with the sonar and plunged into its inky waters, two at a time, in the submarine, until the ITN accounts department called a halt.

All they got for the money were some murky shots yet *News at Ten*'s pictures were syndicated round the world. Monster fever spread as far as Japan. Indeed those pictures still sell today. One American tried to get in on the act by shipping in his own yellow

The submarine used by ITN during one of its attempts to find the Loch Ness Monster. Richard Lindley, pictured right, was one of the reporters who covered the hunt for 'Nessie'.

submarine to sail through the loch, but almost drowned in the attempt. By the end of the expedition no monster had been sighted. All that had been

Leonard Parkin

Leonard Parkin was proud of his image as the archetypal English gentleman. With his film-star good looks and air of unflappability, he was one of ITN's most popular newscasters.

His distinguished career began in his native Yorkshire as a journalist on weekly and evening newspapers before joining the BBC as a television news reporter in 1954. From 1963 to 1965 he was the BBC's Washington correspondent and then a reporter for *Panorama*.

He joined ITN in 1967 and was one of the original team of *News at Ten* newscasters. In 1975 he moved to ITN's *News at One*, which he presented for three years. He moved to *News at 5.45* in 1978 before returning to the *News at One* chair to succeed Peter Sissons.

In addition to newscasting, Leonard Parkin travelled widely for ITN, reporting from the Middle East, covering the Indian emergency of 1972, the American elections of the same year and the French presidential elections of 1980.

After twenty years at ITN Leonard retired from newscasting in 1987. He continued to work in television, making an annual documentary series – *Pieces of Parkin* – in Yorkshire where he was able to pursue his passion for flyfishing.

Leonard died in September 1993 at the age of sixty-four after a long battle with cancer of the spine.

A cholera epidemic in Bengal killed thousands of Pakistanis in refugee camps. They had fled to India to escape attacks by the army during Pakistan's civil war.

found were parts of an old Spitfire engine and what appeared to be some ancient muskets, but they were too slippery for the submarine's grabs to hold. Not to be defeated, Don brought the expedition to a close by telling a news conference that *News at Ten* had now exclusively established as a historical fact that the Monster of Loch Ness did not exist.

From the depths to the heights: *News at Ten* had an early tip-off about the Russian *Soyuz II* space mission – and this time the news was all too grimly conclusive. Amateur space expert Geoff Perry, who had lent his skills to *News at Ten* before, predicted that the mission would end in tragedy. Geoff was monitoring the heartbeats of the cosmonauts by attaching a biro to his short wave radio which was tuned to the output of the spacecraft. Suddenly the biro began drawing a straight line – suggesting that the cosmonauts had died. ITN carried the story that night. The following morning the Russians announced that three men had been killed on re-entry after leaving earth's orbit.

Keeping track of camera crews can be a tricky business – though the logistics are rather more down

to earth, and confusion can have its light side. In the 1970s an ITN assignments manager called Freddie Partington was in charge. One day, cameraman Peter Brown was trying to get through to him on the phone. 'Hello, Peter,' said Freddie. 'I'm on the other line just at the moment. Where are you calling from?' 'Salisbury,' said Peter. 'I shan't be a minute,' said Freddie, putting Peter on hold and going back to his first call. A good five minutes later he finished and picked up the line to Peter. 'Sorry about that,' he said to Peter. 'But tell me, what are you doing in Salisbury? I thought you were abroad.' 'I am,' said Peter. 'You sent me here – Salisbury, Rhodesia.'

The summer's Glastonbury Music Festival set the tone for festivals to come: bad drumming and mud!

And Finally...

Prince Charles tried a bit of gamesmanship when he took part in a charity cricket match at Cranwell RAF College.

He arrived for his innings against Lords Taverners on horseback. However, he decided to dismount before taking up his position at the crease. The horse was led away and Prince Charles scored ten runs before being bowled out.

1972

VIETNAM IS OFTEN referred to as the first television war, not least perhaps because television pictures in homes across America allowed viewers in the 1960s and 1970s to see for themselves what was going on. It was public opinion – formed on the basis of those pictures – that eventually led to the United States withdrawing its ground forces. However, by today's standards the process by which the pictures reached television screens in Britain was rather convoluted. The film had to be carried from the front line and then put on a plane to Hong Kong. Only then could it be sent by satellite back to America and then on to London.

ITN cameraman Alan Downes captured one of the most famous images of the Vietnamese war. Alan's pictures of Kim Phuc showed the world the horror of the war as she ran down the road screaming from a napalm attack.

The dramatic sequence of pictures, taken by ITN cameraman Alan Downes, were to become some of the most memorable images of the Vietnamese war. They showed nine-year-old Kim Phuc, as she ran away from the horror of an American napalm attack. Other children were also caught up in it. The ITN crew were able to give Kim some small comfort.

The war did provide one lighter moment round the *News at Ten* desk as reporter Robert Southgate prepared to fly out to Vietnam on his first assignment there. Foreign editor John Mahoney was discussing arrangements for the trip with Robert when they noticed that Sandy Gall – an experienced Vietnam reporter – was presenting that night's programme. John suggested that Robert should talk to Sandy to get the benefit of his first-hand experience. In those days Sandy and Leonard Parkin took it in turns to do a month of reporting – from Vietnam or some other war-zone – followed by a month of newscasting. Robert approached Sandy and said he was off to Saigon in the morning. He explained that he had done as much reading and research as he could but wondered if Sandy had any advice that would help him when he got there. Straightaway Sandy picked up a pen and paper and said, 'I'll draw it for you, dear boy.' And these were his instructions: 'This is the famous Continental Hotel in downtown Saigon. That's where we always stay along with the rest of the international press. You come out of the door and across the famous terrace where Graham Greene used to have a drink. You go over the main street, turn left, go right, turn left again, walk straight ahead. Then you come to Mr Singh's shop. He's my tailor. Nip in and order a couple of bush jackets. Don't get any of that jungle green colour. It makes you too much of a potential target. Get yourself a nice shade of light blue or even pink.'

If that was the lighter side of Sandy's life as a foreign correspondent, his assignment to Uganda was one of the darkest moments of his reporting career. In August Uganda's bloodthirsty president, General Idi Amin, ordered the expulsion of all Asians holding British passports – about 40,000 people. Later he threw out all Asians, even if they were Ugandan citizens. Sandy was newscasting one night when the foreign editor asked him if he'd like to go and cover the story. Sandy wasn't keen to go but when he was told there was no one else he agreed. His co-operation almost cost him his life.

His first encounter with Idi Amin came, strangely enough, at the hotel where Sandy was staying – the International – a couple of days after Sandy had sent his first report on the Asian expulsion. President Amin had come to the hotel to host a lunch for Uganda's Olympic team who had just returned after the Munich Olympic Games. Sandy and his cameraman approached him at the top table. 'Good afternoon, President Amin,' said Sandy. 'This must be a very proud day for you, having all your Olympic team here.' Amin glared and grunted. Sandy tried again. This time the President turned to the aide next to him and said, 'Get these people out of here.'

Sandy could see he wasn't likely to be getting an interview with Amin and wondered whether he should return to London. The foreign editor at ITN said to wait for a couple of days, giving Sandy the chance to go on a weekend safari – for work, of course. While Sandy and his crew were having lunch at Murchison Falls on the Nile, the restaurant manager told him of radio reports that there'd been an invasion from across the Tanzanian border. When he got back to his hotel he saw two British reporters under arrest in the foyer. They were taken away in a police van.

The next morning Sandy heard Ugandan radio blame both Tanzania and Britain for the invasion. The Ugandan government warned its people to be on the lookout for British spies – military men who could be posing as civilians. Sandy knew it was now time to get out of the country. He was just finishing the script for his safari report when there was a knock at the door. An African man, probably ex-Special Branch and British-trained, Sandy thought, began to question him. When he didn't get the answers he wanted, the man told Sandy to come with him to his headquarters to be questioned by his superiors. He told Sandy to bring his things. It was obviously going to be more than a few questions. Sandy was ordered into a car that was waiting outside the hotel. Already in the car was a young English reporter – Nick Moore – from the Reuters News Agency in Nairobi.

They were taken to a military barracks and ordered into the guardroom. 'Sit down,' barked the corporal in charge. When Nick Moore said there was nothing to sit on, a second soldier hit him across the side of his head with a truncheon. Once their possessions had been removed, the corporal shouted and a younger, bigger soldier appeared. The younger soldier shouted something. 'He wants us to run,' said Nick, who could understand what the soldier was saying. When Sandy hesitated, the soldier hit him with his FN rifle. Sandy ran. The soldier hit Sandy again to make him run faster and Sandy gasped with pain. There were four excruciating blows in all. They kept running until they approached a club-wielding officer. Sandy thought he too was going to start hitting him and tried to explain that he and Nick were journalists who had done nothing wrong. The officer, a major, nodded towards a line of huts and

Andrew Gardner and Reginald Bosanquet – the most enduring partnership of the early days of *News at Ten* – presenting the programme.

pushed Sandy and Nick inside one marked C-19. The door was locked and they realized then they were definitely prisoners. There were a number of African prisoners in there too. There were bullet holes in the walls – about waist-high. The ceiling was splashed with blood that looked quite recent. It was clear that someone had been killed in their cell and not too long ago.

A short while later, four other prisoners came in carrying a fifth who was obviously badly injured. They placed him on the floor and left. The guard caught Sandy's eye and evidently had a change of mind. He called the prisoners back in and ordered them to pick up the wounded man again and take him to another cell. 'The door was locked again,' remembers Sandy, 'and after a minute or two I heard a curious thumping sound, like a hammer or a club hitting something soft. It sounded as if they had been hitting the wounded man.' Sandy was told later that many prisoners at the military barracks were beaten to death with 28-pound hammers. Sandy and Nick now began to think they were going to be killed. 'I felt sick with fear,' says Sandy, 'and I began to pray.'

Later that afternoon a group of officers and soldiers entered the cell and started attacking one of the other prisoners – kicking and pushing him. Then an officer turned to Sandy and asked him who he was. Sandy explained and wrote down his name and who he was working for. The soldiers left but returned to Sandy's cell an hour later and ordered him and Nick to follow him. Sandy wasn't sure what was going to happen next. Were they about to be questioned, beaten up or even killed? They were pushed into a hut with seven other men. One of them was *Sunday Times* photographer Don McCullin, whom Sandy knew. One of the men told Sandy and Nick what a lucky escape the two had had. Cell C-19 was the execution room, as Sandy had suspected.

Shortly after Sandy arrived in the new hut, which was divided into six small rooms with a wash-basin and lavatory at one end, he had a visitor. It was the manager of the International Hotel, where Sandy had been staying. He had realised something bad had happened and managed to track Sandy down on the pretext of getting him to settle the outstanding bill for his room. Sandy played along and managed to give the hotel manager ITN's telex number.

A few days later a soldier came to the hut and began calling out names including Sandy, Nick and Don. It was soon clear they were being released. Sandy was escorted to his hotel to collect his things and then taken to Kampala airport. It was a hot night but inside the plane it was cool. A stewardess offered Sandy a drink. He asked for champagne to celebrate surviving such a frightening ordeal.

'Oh, we don't normally serve champagne in economy,' said the stewardess. 'But wait a moment, let me ask the captain.' She was back in a minute. 'The captain is sending down some champagne with his compliments,' she said.

And Finally...

In the competitive world of sport, women's lib made a major breakthrough. After 400 years of exclusion, women were finally allowed to take part in the World Marbles Championships at Crawley, Sussex.

1973

THE YOM KIPPUR WAR was a turning point for *News at Ten*, as television became people's primary source of news – ahead of radio and, more importantly, newspapers. On Yom Kippur, the holiest day of the Jewish calendar, Israeli soldiers had been praying in their bunkers as their double-fronted war against both Egypt and Syria escalated. Unbeknown to the Israelis, Egyptian troops were building pontoons across the Suez Canal. When they crossed the canal they took the Israelis completely by surprise. At the same time, Syrian forces invaded the Golan Heights and advanced into Israeli-held territory. Israeli troops were mobilized from synagogues; and Israeli radio, which doesn't usually broadcast on Yom Kippur, took to the air to give instructions on where the troops were needed.

In the following days, Israeli troops retook the Golan Heights from the Syrians. The push to win back

An Israeli self-propelled gun on the move during the Yom Kippur war (top). ITN reporter Michael Nicholson reporting from Israeli positions on the Golan Heights (above). Gerald Seymour with Israeli troops, fifteen miles inside the Syrian border (left). Michael and Gerald's reports were sent back to London by satellite and broadcast on the same day they were filmed.

Andrew Gardner watching as Reggie Bosanquet rehearses a live studio interview.

Trevor McDonald joined ITN from the BBC's World Service, aged thirty-three.

territory from the Egyptians turned into a huge and bloody tank battle along the Suez Canal. *News at Ten*'s coverage by reporters Michael Nicholson and Gerald Seymour was sent by satellite back to London. As a result, for the first time viewers could see the pictures of a major foreign news story on the day they'd been filmed and therefore a day ahead of reading about them in the newspapers. Television had at last overtaken newspaper reporting.

A month earlier, a face that was to play a big part in the future of *News at Ten* had arrived at ITN. A thirty-three-year-old Trinidadian named Trevor McDonald left the BBC's World Service radio to become ITN's first black reporter.

Whatever the story, and whatever the pressure of appearing live, *News at Ten* newscasters would always maintain an outward calm. A clue to their real feelings was revealed by some research done in December. Andrew Gardner was wired up with a heart monitor. Just before the programme started it showed Andrew's heart rate rise from a normal seventy-three beats a minute to one hundred and ten.

And Finally...

Computers are wonderful things for saving time, money and large amounts of paper, but they can still have their moments of madness.

The computer for the South Eastern Gas Board sent a quarterly demand to itself. When no payment was forthcoming, it sent a reminder and then the usual threat to disconnect parts of itself if payment was still not forthcoming.

Unfortunately, the reluctant customer receiving these demands was the Gas Board's own show house in Croydon. Someone had entered it as a paying customer.

The Gas Board decided that rather than cut off the supply, they'd remove the house from the records.

Sir Alastair Burnet

Alastair Burnet was the leading newscaster on the first night of *News at Ten* on 3 July 1967. His last night on the programme was twenty-four years later in 1991 when he retired.

Alastair, who was born in Edinburgh in 1928 and educated at Leys School, Cambridge, and Worcester College, Oxford, originally joined ITN in 1963 as political editor. He was then appointed editor of *The Economist* from 1965 until 1974. It was during this period that he returned to ITN to be the leading newscaster of *News at Ten* for the programme's three-month trial. He continued working for ITN on and off until 1972 when he started presenting *Panorama* for the BBC. In 1974 he moved from *The Economist* to become the editor of the *Daily Express* for the next two years.

He rejoined ITN in 1976 as a newscaster for the *News at 5.45* and later moved back to the position of senior newscaster on *News at Ten*. He was also an ITN board member and associate editor of *News at Ten* as well as being an independent national director of *The Times*.

He was the anchorman for major ITN programmes including the Apollo space missions, general elections and budgets. In 1981 he was one of the two main commentators for the royal wedding of Prince Charles and Lady Diana Spencer and, in 1982, the commentator for the ITV network for the visit to Britain of Pope John Paul II. In 1984, he anchored ITN's special programmes on the D-Day celebrations and the US presidential election.

In 1985 his exclusive interview for ITN with the Prince and Princess of Wales was watched by more than 18 million people in Britain and was shown around the world. The following year he presented ITN's special two-part programme, *In Private... In Public – The Prince and Princess of Wales*, a unique behind-the-scenes view of the royal couple.

In January 1988 he anchored ITN's coverage of

Australia's bicentennial celebrations in a live television spectacular from Sydney. He was involved in another historical event when he presented ITN's programmes on President and Mrs Gorbachev's visit to Britain in 1989.

He is the author of four books: *The ITN Book of the Queen Mother*, *In Person – The Prince and Princess of Wales*, *The ITN Book of the Royal Wedding*, and *In Private...In Public – The Prince and Princess of Wales*.

Alastair Burnet's professional abilities have been officially recognized many times. He was awarded the Richard Dimbleby Award from BAFTA in 1966, 1970 and 1979. In 1982 he received the Royal Television Society Judges' Prize and in 1970 he was named Political Broadcaster of the year. He was knighted in the 1984 New Year's Honours List for his services to journalism and broadcasting.

1974

The Turkish invasion of Cyprus produced one of *News at Ten*'s most memorable pieces of film – one of those magic moments when planning, luck, and impromptu genius combine. Trying to get pictures of the invasion had been logistically difficult. ITN – like the BBC – had several crews on the island. Communication with London and flights to and from Cyprus were almost impossible. In the meantime in the *News at Ten* studio in London, Peter Snow had been explaining the war with models and diagrams, as the coup against the island's President, Archbishop Makarios, unfolded.

Turkish paratroopers were expected to land on the coast – providing the pictures that the world's news organizations had been waiting for. ITN reporter Michael Nicholson and his crew set off for the coast but, as luck would have it, their car broke down. They managed to enlist the help of an English-speaking student who knew of ITN from his days in Britain. Then they heard the drone of aircraft engines – the Turks weren't landing their paratroopers on the coast after all. The newsmen found themselves actually in the middle of the drop zone.

Then came the moment of television history. A thousand Turkish paras dropped on to the island, and waiting below them were Michael and his crew. As they landed around him, Michael made the most of his opportunity. He ran up to the bemused Turks and began to interview them with the now immortal words, 'I'm Michael Nicholson of ITN. Welcome to Cyprus.' It had been one of ITN's finest hours.

Michael Nicholson found himself in the drop zone for the Turkish invasion of Cyprus in July where he greeted surprised paratroopers.

But that wasn't quite the end of the story. The film was placed on an RAF Comet plane which was returning to Britain. It didn't arrive at ITN until 7.00pm the following evening. That left three hours

A Turkish soldier staking his country's claim to Cyprus.

to develop, edit and dub the film – quite a tall order in those days. Some of it was still being edited and dubbed as *News at Ten* went on the air.

The *News at Ten* studio director Diana Edwards-Jones became the first woman to direct an election night television programme in February – and her success was recognized by the Royal Television Society for outstanding creative achievement behind the camera.

In April, News *at Ten* showed world-exclusive pictures of Adolf Hitler's deputy, Rudolf Hess, filmed secretly inside Spandau jail in Berlin. It was taken by a former American commandant at the jail, Colonel Eugene Bird. Hess had been sentenced to life imprisonment at the Nuremberg trials after the Second World War and had been held inside Spandau jail ever since. In 1974 he was seventy-nine years old, and he was the last inmate in the jail that was built to house 600 prisoners. The pictures were the first anyone had seen of him for twenty-eight years.

ITN found itself in difficulties with the courts over film shown on *News at Ten* of clashes that took place in Red Lion Square in central London. They involved on the one side the National Front, which had arranged a march, and on the other the civil rights group Liberation which held a counter demonstration. A student died in the violence. The courts wanted ITN pictures to be made available to help the police in their investigation. ITN said it would hand over only the film that had been broadcast on the television because that was available to everyone. It didn't want to release the long sequences that had been edited out because journalists and camera crews could be placed at risk in similar situations if demonstrators thought they were agents for the police. In the end, it was a battle that ITN lost. The courts ordered the extra film to be handed over.

In June, a chemical factory at Flixborough on Humberside exploded, spewing acid everywhere and killing twenty-nine people who worked there. When news started coming through, the ITN newsroom was rather empty. It was supper time and there was something of a carnival going on in nearby Charlotte Street in the West End. The only two people in the newsroom were news editor Mark Andrews and a new scriptwriter called Sam Hall. The two had hardly met one another before. Mark asked Sam if he'd ever done any reporting. Sam said no. 'Well, now's your chance,' said Mark. Sam was sent to Elstree, by taxi, to get into a helicopter and fly to Flixborough, where a local camera crew would meet him. The taxi had just pulled away from ITN House when Sam saw reporter Keith Hatfield returning from the carnival. Sam pulled him into the car and they headed for the waiting helicopter.

Soon they were airborne. Fifty miles away from Flixborough they saw the sky was bright orange. They knew then just what a big story it was going to be. When they arrived all that remained of the chemical factory was the charred metal framework – like a giant skeleton. The explosion was so powerful that people in Scunthorpe, four miles away, were thrown to the ground. About a hundred stone-built houses near the factory had been wrecked. With Sam as his producer, Keith Hatfield filed his report for that

Gordon Honeycombe on the *News at Ten* set. The chroma-key window over his shoulder is blank. The image of Edward Heath which appears on the monitor on the right appears in its correct position on the monitor in the centre.

night's programme. But their work wasn't over. Keith wanted to find someone from the factory to interview.

Eventually, after all the other reporters had left the scene, the works manager turned up, looking, not surprisingly, totally shattered. In the dead of night he confided that he thought a broken pipe was the problem. Another section of pipe had been fitted to by-pass the break and he believed there had been a faulty join. That caused a build-up of chemical vapour that triggered the accident. The next day Keith's report contained this exclusive new information. A year later, the inquiry into the disaster confirmed what the works manager had said, and what ITN had reported.

There was an amusing finale to the trip, despite the gravity of the story. Sam still only had the clothes he stood up in. Fully fledged reporters like Keith always keep an overnight bag with them. Sam had decided he would try and get the creases out of his trousers by hanging them over the shower rail. The inevitable

happened and they fell into the water. Sam had to borrow Keith's spare pair. Sam is five feet seven inches tall. Keith is over six feet. Sam went off to secure an important interview wearing a pair of trousers rolled up to his ankles.

Reporter Norman Rees also had a sudden summons to duty, though this one took him to the other side of the world. He was just settling down for a family Christmas when there was a call from the foreign desk asking him to catch a flight to Melbourne. The runaway Labour MP John Stonehouse had just been arrested by Australian police. It was an amazing story. Stonehouse was a former Postmaster General, a high-profile member of Parliament. Earlier that year his clothes had been found on a beach in Miami. He had disappeared, and the two possibilities were suicide or accidental drowning. Details emerged of his business life which suggested he had been in some kind of financial trouble.

His arrest meant, of course, that he had carried out an elaborate fake. He had managed to obtain a new passport and had been living under a false name in Australia. The police had been put onto him by a bank teller who had become suspicious over some of his transactions.

Norman remembers that day: 'It was goodbye Christmas, hello Australia. What I hadn't quite realized is that nobody wants to travel to Australia the day before Christmas. You take off on Christmas Eve and land on Boxing Day. Not ideal if you are visiting family or friends.' At the check-in desk there were seven or eight other passengers. Every one of them was another journalist. Norman says: 'We had a jumbo jet virtually to ourselves and were determined to party. The cabin crew were terrific and by the end we were helping in the galley serving Christmas lunch to them!'

Norman was to make three trips to Australia on the Stonehouse story. By contrast to his first journey out, the final trip back was a nightmare. Scotland Yard had just won an extradition order and had travelled to pick John Stonehouse up from a detention centre to bring him back for trial. ITN had done a deal with the Yard that if Stonehouse agreed to talk to Norman on the flight they would not interfere.

The intention was to get off the plane in Hong Kong to send the pictures back to London by satellite. Because of the time difference the story would make that night's *News at Ten* ahead of the plane's arrival in London the next morning. Within minutes of takeoff Norman had a problem. John Stonehouse, in surprisingly good humour, immediately gave an interview to the BBC. Then, out of the blue, his mood changed. He had once had a major bust-up with the chairman of a certain ITV company and there was no way that he would give an interview to ITN.

The devastation caused by an explosion at a chemical factory at Flixborough on Humberside.

For five miserable hours Norman sweated over the possibility that the BBC would have the story he thought was going to be his. Then just before they were due to land in Hong Kong there was at last a breakthrough.

Norman's Australian cameraman had once given Stonehouse's mistress the use of a flat as a hideaway during one of the many times she was under siege from the Press. 'You may not owe anything to ITN, John,' said the cameraman. 'But you certainly owe a return favour to me ...' Stonehouse relented. They got the interview before touch-down. The story was safely in the can and the satellite worked. They had made it.

And Finally...

A Wolverhampton department store sent a letter in the internal post to Mrs Gwen James, who worked at that time in the crockery department. It was addressed to G. D. James, 36312, which was her staff number.

Unfortunately, the letter somehow got into the external mail by mistake and it finally reached her two months later ... via Peking.

1975

THE THIRTY-YEAR WAR in Vietnam ended when the South Vietnamese capital Saigon surrendered almost without a fight as the North Vietnamese tanks streamed into the city and knocked down the gates of the presidential palace. Lorries full of cheering Communist troops drove through Saigon. But there remained among most of the population a terrible fear of the Communists and what they would do. Thousands of people tried to leave Saigon by boat, but had to turn back when North Vietnamese tanks fired across their bows.

One of the most memorable scenes of those days was the closure of the American Embassy and the chaos that surrounded the withdrawal of the last American diplomats, foreigners, well-connected Vietnamese and US troops. Thousands of people swarmed around the embassy, trying to get on to the helicopters that were shuttling from the roof of the embassy to the relative safety of American warships in the South China Sea. Among those scrambling to get aboard the helicopters were ITN's Michael Nicholson and his crew, cameraman Peter Wilkinson and soundman Hugh Thomson. The last eleven marines of the unit which had been guarding the embassy were lifted from the roof when an angry mob started firing, and when it became clear that the helicopters had made their last flights, the mob ransacked the Embassy.

Sandy Gall was reporting from Vietnam at the same time. Both had planned to come out on those last

Michael Nicholson and his sound recordist Hugh Thomson being helped over the gates of the American Embassy in Saigon by US Marines before they were flown out of the city.

flights but it didn't quite work out like that. Sandy had witnessed the earlier evacuation of the British Embassy. Just as he was waving off the Consul, Sandy

The Evacuation of the American Embassy in Saigon, 2 May 1975

The docks on Tuesday morning were crammed with thousands of Vietnamese desperate to escape from Saigon by any means possible. Large old American landing craft had been filled with more than a thousand people who were going to attempt the impossible: try and sail down the river to the sea.

The harbour was full of small cargo ships, full of people whose only way out now was this desperate, perhaps suicidal, attempt. As we, the press and the Americans evacuating, made our drive through Saigon to the American Embassy, people, mostly families, pleaded with us for a seat and they clung to the coach.

The coach behind us suddenly accelerated and children hanging on the side fell off and under the wheels. The city was suddenly choked with people - lorries and cars all chasing one American evacuation convoy after another - jams that the Vietnamese police tried to clear with their rifles but people were no longer afraid of them. There was now so much more to be afraid of.

But then suddenly we too, forty or fifty of us in the safety of the coaches, had to get out to fight our way to the American compound where helicopters were landing to fly us and the thousands more out of the country.

Seeing us in the streets with our bags, the Vietnamese followed - any chance, they thought, was better than none. But the embassy gates were closed and we, like the frightened Vietnamese and their families, had to fight and claw our way up. And we did claw and we did fight and if it wasn't for one single American marine whose name I didn't have the chance or time to discover, we would never have climbed our way to our evacuation. He hauled us up, kicking and punching Vietnamese, who were clambering over our bodies.

Ashamed and exhausted, we took our turn in the long crowd of refugees inside the embassy compound and waited for the embassy helicopters to come down for us. One by one they came in, landing on an improvised pad in the car park. All had come from American aircraft carriers twenty miles out in the South China Sea.

Marines guarded each of the four embassy gates as the lucky people ran thirty at a time to their transport to safety. In the first six hours of Tuesday, one thousand five hundred people were airlifted out this way and almost as many more were still waiting their turn. Our turn came just as it was starting to get dark, a little after 7.30, evacuees from the besieged city.

And thirty minutes later we landed safely on our carrier on the South Vietnamese coast.

Michael Nicholson, *News at Ten*, USS Hancock, South China Sea.

Sandy Gall reporting from the Vietnamese capital Saigon as the victorious North Vietnamese troops enter the city.

joked that he could run the Embassy Club with its bar and restaurant as a press club now the Consul was going. To Sandy's surprise the Consul, Rex Hunt, later to be Governor of the Falklands said, 'Sandy, what a very good idea,' and handed the keys to him.

Later, when it was obvious Saigon was going to fall, Sandy and Michael both headed to the meeting point for the flights out. When they found out that a BBC crew was staying, it put things in rather a different light. The French crew that had been working for ITN in Vietnam decided they were going to stay, partly rather than give the competition the upper hand but also because, being French, they wouldn't get such a hard time from the North Vietnamese as a British or American crew. Naturally, a reporter had to stay with them. As Michael had been in Vietnam several weeks earlier than Sandy, it was agreed he would be first out.

Sandy and his French crew filmed the amazing scenes of North Vietnamese tanks and then infantry confirming their hold on Saigon. Communication with London was difficult because the North Vietnamese had cut all telephone and telex links with the outside world. There was no way of sending out any of the film. Telex lines only re-opened after a press conference by the victorious North

Vietnamese general. Sandy could now send messages and scripts back to ITN, but could do nothing about the mounting pile of film cans. The answer was a plane. Sandy approached the general and suggested that the only way ITN's film of his triumphal arrival in Saigon could be seen by the outside world would be if the general could supply an aircraft to send it on.

Two weeks and two days after the fall of Saigon, Sandy was told he would be flown out the next day. He went to the airport only to be told the flight had been cancelled. The flight out came the following week. Among Sandy's luggage was the precious film of the fall of Saigon. He feared the North Vietnamese officials might take it from him as he boarded the plane out, but they didn't. He and eighty others crammed into the Russian Ilyushin plane that took off for Vientiane, the capital of Laos.

There a cargo plane chartered by ITN picked up Sandy to fly him to Bangkok, in Thailand. When Sandy arrived he was feted by his American colleagues and plied with champagne. Then another American, whom Sandy hadn't met before, approached him. The man said he had bad news. Sandy thought of his wife and children, but it was

ITN's Geoffrey Archer on board a mercy flight bringing Vietnamese orphans to Britain in April.

nothing like that. 'ITV is on strike,' the American said. It meant Sandy's remarkable report didn't appear on *News at Ten* for a few more days – one month after the fall of Saigon.

High above the earth friendship was breaking out between the two Cold War enemies – the United States and the Soviet Union. An American Apollo spacecraft and a Soviet Soyuz joined up in space 140 miles up. The commanders of each mission shook hands through the open hatches of their two crafts and then the astronauts and the cosmonauts moved around from one to the other. They carried out joint experiments and had a meal together.

ITN had co-opted a grammar school headmaster from Kettering, Geoff Perry, as a space adviser. One of Geoff's early triumphs was to crack the code used by the Soviet Union for transmitting messages to and from space. He came to realize, by humming out

Andrew Gardner and Reginald Bosanquet sharing a joke on the *News at Ten* set. Behind them is the chroma-key window where the key images of the day's news could be projected.

loud, that each transmission began in roughly the same way. He guessed correctly that each coded message must start with the time in Moscow. From that he was able to work out exactly what was going on during the Soviet space programme.

Early reports about the 1975 rendezvous suggested the good-will handshake would take place over Moscow. ITN didn't believe the Americans would allow such an obvious propaganda coup, so contacted Geoff. He used one of his school globes, driven by a clockwork motor to simulate the earth's rotation, together with the charts of the orbits of the two spacecraft. He calculated they would meet somewhere over the English Channel. At ITN, the

The scene inside one of the carriages at the Moorgate tube train disaster – the worst in the history of London Underground. Thirty-four passengers and the driver died when the train rammed into a dead-end tunnel in February.

At the last moment there was a new chill in the thawing relations between America and the Soviet Union and the Russians refused to climb into the tunnel between the two spacecraft. The Americans, they said, would have to make the first move. Sadly for Bognor, the time it took to resolve just who was going to move first meant the locked craft had drifted over Northern France by the time the historic handshake took place.

exact place was pinpointed. It would be off the Sussex coast a few miles south of Bognor. ITN made much of the story that the handshake would be just off the British coast. NASA confirmed Geoff had got his sums right. As the Soyuz was blasted into orbit from its launch site at Baikonur the newspaper headlines in Britain read, 'Bognor, here we come!'

And Finally...

In Manchester, a former human cannonball rose from the grave. Blondini, whose real name was Mike Costello, had volunteered to be buried alive in an attempt to break the world record. When he eventually emerged, seventy-eight days, one hour and five minutes later, the record was his, along with a cheque for £500.

Mike had been entombed in a glass-topped coffin and, for the sum of 10p each, people could come and see him. 'Perhaps,' said the daredevil, 'some of them were depressed and seeing my circumstances cheered them up.'

1976

SANDY GALL FOUND HIMSELF in a Spanish jail in January when he went to report on the widespread strikes by postal, railway and car workers. Sandy and his American cameraman were outside the gates of the Chrysler factory in Madrid, filming some employees who were trying to get past a group of pickets to return to work. At first Sandy was questioned and then led away in handcuffs to be interrogated at a police station in the centre of Madrid where he and his team had to remove their watches, belts and shoelaces. It was only when an official from the Ministry of Information and Tourism arrived with a form ordering their release that they managed to avoid a spell in the cells.

Norman Rees reporting on the Cod War from on board the Icelandic gunboat the *Thor*. In the background is HMS *Leander*, part of the Royal Navy protection force.

Iceland had stunned the United Kingdom by suddenly announcing a fifty-mile exclusion zone on foreign fishermen in the seas around Iceland. This followed warnings from their marine scientists of rapidly depleting fish stocks – Iceland's major source of income. At that time hundreds of trawlers from Grimsby, Hull and other British deep-sea ports regularly sailed to Iceland, their traditional fishing grounds, searching for shoals of cod. Faced with stiff quotas at best or, much worse, total exclusion, Britain's deep-sea fleet faced ruin.

The Icelanders began enforcing the ban by deploying their small fleet of gunboats. These began cutting the nets of trawlers, costing the skippers and their owners thousands of pounds in lost catches and equipment. To defend the fleet Britain deployed a number of frigates. The Cod War had begun.

Reporter Norman Rees was sent to Iceland to cover the story. It was to be a difficult assignment. The British trawlers could be dispersed anywhere around Iceland's coastline. The confrontations were sporadic and unpredictable. The ITN team spent hours in chartered light aircraft trying to track events, and days at sea on chartered Icelandic vessels looking for the action. But after months of diplomatic negotiations they hit the jackpot. The Iceland government allowed the ITN crew on to one of their gunboats. At last Norman could guarantee to be with the action and to see it from a unique perspective – with the enemy.

The collision of *Thor* and HMS *Leander*.

And it wasn't just any gunboat. The skipper of the *Thor*, Captain Helgi Hallvardson, had already been nicknamed 'The Mad Dog' by British fishermen because of his particularly persistent and daring raids. Norman recalls: 'When we first got on board it was made plain that not every member of the crew was happy with the decision to let us on. And in only a few hours we were in trouble – deep trouble.'

They spent their free time sailing out to the fishing grounds by picking up lots of general shots around the boat. 'We thought a great view would be looking down at the bow cutting through the waves from up in the crow's nest,' says Norman. ' The trouble was it had a slightly scratched Perspex window which spoiled the shot. But just above was a hatch. Looking out through there, I thought, would be perfect. As I opened it up there was an almighty crash and the hatch was practically wrenched from its solid steel hinges.'

It transpired that it was the inspection hatch for the ship's radar arm, only to be opened when the radar was switched off. The rotating antenna had smashed into the hatch and both were locked solid. 'I now had to go down to tell the Icelandic officers on the bridge why the radar screens searching for the British trawlers had suddenly gone blank and why they were

now sailing blind. Not a pleasant experience,' says Norman. 'We were so obviously and acutely embarrassed that I think they took pity on us.'

The radar proved relatively easy to fix and within a day or two they had their confrontation at sea. It turned into a chase on the high seas as a British frigate moved in at speed to protect fishing gear that *Thor* was determined to cut. It ended with a stomach-churning collision between gunboat and warship that left both vessels damaged.

They had pictures illustrating the reality of the Cod War which were better than they could have imagined. In those days there was no way to send them by satellite out of Iceland and they put the pictures on a plane.

'They had a huge play on *News at Ten* – but an even bigger play in Iceland. They were run practically every hour on the hour,' says Norman.

To the viewers at home it was evidence of the Royal Navy doing a sterling job protecting British fishermen from unnecessary and unlawful aggression. The Icelanders, however, saw it as their tiny outweighed, outgunned coastguard ship

The Queen celebrates her fiftieth birthday by appearing in front of the cameras with Prince Edward and Prince Phillip.

taking on the might of the Royal Navy and giving it a bloody nose.

Captain Hallvardson and his crew were the heroes of the Cod War. When Norman and the ITN crew got back to Reykjavik there were dignitaries, a brass band and a local television crew waiting. Norman says: 'We were invited to join *Thor*'s crew as they were feted on the quayside. I decided it wouldn't be a good idea for an ITN team to be seen joining the Icelandic celebrations over a bang with a British frigate, so we stayed below deck until it all went quiet.'

Hallvardson turned out to be quite an affable man when he was off the bridge. He and Norman stayed in touch for many years. Norman says: 'Before I left Reykjavik he presented me with a polished brass shell from the gunboat's ancient cannon,' says Norman.

In the early stages of the Cod War BBC and ITN camera crews took it in turns to patrol with the Royal Navy. There was what's called a 'pool' arrangement – where one crew made available their pictures to the other broadcaster. On one occasion the BBC sent ITN three cans of dramatic film. Picture editor Gordon Hickey cut together a nine-minute report for *News at Ten* which was voiced by reporter Keith Hatfield. The BBC only ran a one-and-a-half-minute report on their *Nine O'Clock News*, using the same material. The BBC cameraman went on to win an award for the pictures he shot that day, but he entered the *News at Ten* report, not the one shown on the BBC itself.

A world away from cold northern seas, *News at Ten*'s Jon Snow was in Uganda to interview General Idi Amin, who had seized power some years earlier and was now quarrelling with Kenya. The General's reputation as a tyrant and a murdering bully set the nerves of the crew somewhat on edge. Jon for his part had already become known as a reporter who asked penetrating questions. His crew – cameraman Derek Seymour and sound recordist Tony Piddington – were worried that Amin already looked pretty

General Idi Amin – the tyrannical President of Uganda – caused an ITN crew a few heart-stopping moments during their interview with him.

irascible and a few probing questions from Jon might push him over the edge.

Just as Jon started the interview Derek moved his camera slightly to improve the shot. In doing so, he pulled the cable that connected the camera to the sound recorder and dislodged a vital plug. Soundman Tony didn't notice at first. When he did realize, he pushed the plug back in with trembling hands. Fortunately the best of the interview was yet to come. As Tony said later, 'I could tell this Amin chap wasn't in any mood to be asked to repeat what he'd said.'

Meanwhile, Alastair Burnet returned to ITN to help launch the newly revamped 5.45pm news programme. Since his first short spell as presenter at the start of *News at Ten* in 1967, he had been editor of the *Economist* magazine and more recently he'd been editor of the *Daily Express*. He would rejoin *News at Ten* the following year, and his association with the programme was to continue – unbroken this time – for the next fourteen years.

All news centres have to be very conscious about security. In the *News at Ten* studios, not only are there frequent visitors by celebrities of all sorts who may

be subjected to unwelcome attention – but the studios themselves may be targeted by people wanting to make a point. One such occasion was in November this year, when five people tried to force their way in just as *News at Ten* was going on air. The invaders – who turned out to be Welsh language protesters – were thrown out after a scuffle.

One distinguished visitor to ITN House around this time was Denis Healey, then Chancellor of the Exchequer. *News at Ten* was regularly reporting his dealings with the International Monetary Fund – he was trying to borrow money to support the pound against foreign currencies. When he came in for his studio interview, he first asked if he could use a phone. Everyone assumed it must be important economic business – perhaps a call to the Governor of the Bank of England suggesting a rise in interest rates or to the IMF to ask about the chances of borrowing more money. Ears were wagging in

News at Ten's most enduring partnership between Andrew Gardner and Reginald Bosanquet draws to a close.

anticipation of getting a major scoop. Mr Healey dialled a number and was then heard to say, 'Hello, Edna. I just thought you'd like to know I'm going to be on the telly in five minutes,' proving that Chancellors are human and like to impress their wives.

And Finally...

On a farm in Holland a vet was called in when a cow's stomach became swollen with gas. The vet put a tube into the cow and then lit a match to test the escaping gas. There was an explosion followed by a fire, which set light to bales of hay and burned the farm to the ground.

The vet and the cow were unharmed.

1977

THE LARGE SPECTRE OF the Ugandan President, General Idi Amin, hung over the news agenda for much of the year. His six-year reign of terror was reaching its most violent phase. There were reports of thousands of killings ordered by Amin. He almost certainly ordered the death of the Archbishop of Uganda and two government ministers. In June *News at Ten* spoke to two Ugandan exiles, a doctor and a vet, who said the General was not only involved in the ritual execution and slaughter of those ministers but in the case of his Minister of Works he drank his blood afterwards. The witnesses said he had dressed up in a white robe for the murder of the Minister of Works and made sure the man had his hands and feet tied. The doctor said Amin was suffering from hallucinations and mental disorders.

In July ITN broadcast its own documentary called *The ITN Story* to mark the tenth anniversary of *News at Ten*. It contained two of Reggie Bosanquet's most embarrassing moments. The first happened when he went to interview strikers outside an engineering factory in the Midlands. He asked a man in a flat cap for his views on the strike. 'It's nothing to do with me, guv'nor,' the man replied bluntly, 'I'm just here selling newspapers.'

The second was when he interviewed the Duke of Edinburgh about a trip he'd made to the United States, helping to promote British exports. Reggie asked him, 'What did the Americans you met think

The country celebrated with the Queen as she marked her Silver Jubilee – twenty-five years as monarch.

of this country?' to which Prince Phillip apparently replied, 'What a stupid question, I didn't ask them all. There are two hundred and fifty million of them.'

Leonard Parkin and Sandy Gall during a light-hearted moment on the *News At Ten* set.

As *News at Ten* celebrated its first decade, one of the founding fathers, Andrew Gardner, who had presented the programme since that first night, announced he was leaving. He was by then forty-four. He took up a job with Thames Television presenting their local evening news programme, *Thames at Six*. It was the end of one of the most famous partnerships in television – Gardner and Bosanquet – and the end of an era.

The death of the King – Elvis Presley – will always stick in the minds of rock 'n' roll fans around the world. That night – 16 August – will also stick in the minds of the *News at Ten* team. About four minutes before the programme was about to finish, news came through from the Associated Press news agency on the tele-printers that Elvis was dead. Reggie read out that reports were coming in of Elvis's death. A minute or so later, another Associated Press report came up on the printer saying Elvis had been taken to hospital – raising the possibility that perhaps he wasn't dead after all. *News at Ten* ended that night with Reggie saying '… and Elvis Presley is dead – or is he?' Straight after the programme checks were made with Associated Press, who explained the confusion. They had issued the report about Elvis being taken to hospital first. When they heard that he had died they released a second report and 'flashed' or prioritized it so it came up before the first one. Reggie went back on the air shortly afterwards to clear up the confusion and confirm the sad news.

Before the year ended, rumours were rife about who might be striking up a new on-screen partnership with Reggie and with Alastair Burnet, who by now

Red Rum back home in Southport after becoming the first horse to win the Grand National three times.

had moved from the 5.45pm news. The name in the frame was Anna Ford. She was the thirty-three-year-old presenter of BBC's *Tomorrow's World* programme.

And Finally...

The footballing regulars of the Wharncliffe Hotel, Barnsley, Yorkshire, voted their goalkeeper 'Player of the Year', despite the fact that he let through 120 goals during the season.

One of his team mates said, 'Without him it would have been much worse. He's the best player in the team.'

Trouble during the Grunwick dispute in June. The film processing plant became the focus for the biggest industrial relations story of the year. Workers, supported by hundreds of students, demonstrated against the company's refusal to have trade unions.

INTERVIEW
Sir Alastair Burnet

'I did Monday, Tuesday and Friday at ITN and I did Wednesday and Thursday at *The Economist*. And I smoked eighty cigarettes a day,' says Sir Alastair Burnet remembering the early days of *News at Ten*.

Alastair Burnet first joined ITN in 1963. He left, then came back in 1967 to become the lead newscaster on *News at Ten* which was to start that July. He continued as editor of *The Economist* and divided his week between print and television journalism for three months.

Alastair still feels passionate about the birth of the programme: 'News was, to our minds, something very much more important than light entertainment. So it required a certain amount of time, a certain amount of dignity, a certain amount of money spent on it, a certain amount of brainpower put into it, a certain amount of attention paid to it. And this really was the first news programme which could claim that all those things were attached to it. The BBC's news before that was zilch. ITN suffered very much from lack of resources and from lack of time. And so *News at Ten* was a very obvious development. It was, for its day, a breakthrough.'

At the end of the first *News at Ten* on 3 July, Alastair asked the nation to change its viewing habits. Apart from the 10.00pm start, what does he believe the viewers got which was so revolutionary?

'The viewers got a coherent and embracing, comprehensive news. The news had always been in very short flashes, very short bits of film which were often out-of-date. The writers and the film crews took advantage of the chance to do five-minute items. ITN had some of the best film crews in the business because they had worked on Pathé and Gaumont and so on. They really rose to the opportunity of doing six or seven minutes instead

of shooting thirty seconds. Equally a little bit more money was spent on bringing in news and actually paying for satellites.'

The change that struck the audience in the very first minute of the first *News at Ten* was seeing Alastair and Andrew Gardner together. Alastair says the concept of two newscasters was 'something that had worked very well in America on the NBC news. The public could decide who was in a good mood, whether they got on and so on.'

He remembers that until *News at Ten*, 'voices' had been employed to read the commentary in reports as they did in cinema news. 'On *News at Ten*, reporters voiced all their own reports, whether it was live or recorded. This was new. ITN had done it in a little way, but by and large they had used the "voices". A lot of television news began in the cinema and it was difficult to shrug off. This technique tended to cauterize the news, it didn't get the human element in the man's or woman's voice.

'The viewers also got a centre-break for advertising, although the advertisers had said nobody could advertise in the news. How wrong they were.

'And they got sport, which we hoped would continue to grab them, and could even be a running theme if there was a big match going on.'

Alastair makes no secret of being a Partick Thistle fan, and he often squeezed in an extra phrase or two while rattling through the football results, such as 'Hearts 1, Rangers 2 – McCoist, of course'. Viewers may have thought his knowledge stemmed from a lifelong love of the game, but he denies this. 'No, no. I don't really like saying this, but most young scriptwriters don't give a damn about sport and treat it with contempt. They are intellectuals. Anybody, like the production assistants, could tell them much more about sport than they wished to know. I felt that if we talked down to people about sport and if we didn't show enthusiasm about it, then we were wasting our time. Therefore, it was quite important to learn the basics of what was happening in the football league. It didn't take very long to learn.'

Was he himself ever keen on sport? 'I was always interested in cricket, I played cricket and rugby when I was at school and hockey when I was at Oxford so I did know a bit about sport. But I didn't really understand much about soccer – but that was what people wanted to know about and it was quite wrong to offer them an inferior sports news.'

When asked what life was like in those pioneering days, he throws his head back and laughs. 'Oh, it was tough, it was tough. Yes, it was fun. They were agreeable people to work with. That was the great thing. It was a team effort. I know people always say, "It's a team effort" but in a newsroom you can tell whether it's a happy place.

And you can tell if they are prepared to argue ... in a good way. Because ITN was doing new things which other people hadn't done, because there was a little bit more money, and above all because there was success – success after the first ten days – they knew they were on a winning run. That bucks people up no end, it really does. And although the prima donnas came along – they'll say I was one and I can understand that – by and large we prima donnas didn't go too far.'

Alastair does not hesitate when asked with whom he most enjoyed presenting *News at Ten*.

'Andrew Gardner – he was a gentleman. Sandy Gall – he was a gentleman.' He gives an inscrutable smile and says: 'I'm not going further.'

Anyone who watched *News at Ten* in its first twenty-five years must have asked at least once: 'What do they say to each other at the end of the programme?' Alastair used to quip that he asked his female co-presenters, 'Your place or mine?', but he now admits: 'You couldn't really say anything because there were lipreaders. And it was difficult to have a good laugh because there might have been some kind of difficult news in the programme. Obviously one didn't want to be disagreeable to anybody. So it was best to pray that they would take the picture off very soon and show us just putting our papers together. We knew that we were going to have a drink – almost all of us – after the programme, which was something to look forward to.'

In the Wells Street building they would usually repair to the ITN Club bar on the sixth floor. 'That was an essential part of life. Sometimes one would go outside, but then that meant there was a conspiracy,' Alastair reminisces. 'These were very, very agreeable days and it was possible, because of the ITN Club, to see people who had done stories and to say, "Well done" quietly. Then it was also possible just to insert the thought after a couple of drinks that a story could have been improved in some way or another. You got hard luck stories and you got excuses.' He chortles: 'And you got people who wanted to read their bits again.'

He continues: 'Therefore, while enjoying the drinking very much, I thought it did have a purpose. At 10.00pm the life of London was running down, and the only place to go was the ITN Club. That worked well. We also didn't have a post mortem right there, which was what the BBC eventually came to do. That must have been hellish – considering the kind of programmes they were putting out.'

In the 1980s the Job Survey was a regular feature on *News at Ten* each Friday night. Dots flashed on a map of the UK indicating the major job losses or gains that week. 'I think it reflected what was happening in a way that the British public had only just come to understand, because for a long time – right from when Heath was Prime Minister – it was absolutely dreadful that there were as many as a million unemployed. People were wringing their hands. Therefore, when unemployment rose to three million, I think it was important in some way to just reflect the seriousness of it. We couldn't reflect the small job losses but we did our best to cover everything over, I think, 100 jobs.

'The Labour party wanted job losses to be higher, the Tory party wanted them to be lower. I think we got the curve right and I would say to this day, obviously there were individual job losses which we didn't include, but we got the trends right and I think we got the seriousness of the unemployment problem right. We were sometimes better than the government's figures. I think it served a very useful purpose. I remember Mrs Thatcher saying, "I shall be happy when you don't have the bloody job losses."'

It was also the decade of *Spitting Image*. Was Alastair hurt by the way he was caricatured? He considers for a moment and replies: 'Not really.

They were earning a living. I didn't mind that at all. It went on, I think, too long. You're daft to take exception to all these things. You've got to be able to take what the newspapers say. You've got to be able to take what television says about you. The important thing is to go on, don't worry about it.

'I felt terribly sorry about poor Lord Steel, though. I suppose if one were representing a political party then it would be pretty nasty. It would denigrate all the people who voted for him. I can see that, but for an old clown like a newscaster, no – I don't think it should matter.'

And finally... Are there any great figures in history that Alastair would have liked to interview for *News at Ten*?

'I'm hoping to interview all these people when I go upstairs – or downstairs,' he contemplates. 'It will be something to do in the millennia that are to come.'

Alastair Burnet taking his appearance in another newspaper cartoon in good humour.

1978

THE ANNOUNCEMENT THAT Anna Ford was indeed joining the *News at Ten* team came in February. At first the BBC said they wouldn't let Anna join – claiming that if she left the BBC to join ITN it would be a breach of her contract. But the wrangle was quickly resolved. Her salary was supposed to be confidential but was widely reported to be £14,000 a year – worth rather more then than it is now. Inevitably, instant comparisons were made with Angela Rippon, who was reading the *Nine O'Clock News* on BBC1 and who was virtually the same age.

To move into the hot seat vacated by Andrew Gardner was a tall order for anyone. ITN wasn't about to take any chances with their most high profile outside signing. So her bosses tried to take some of the pressure off by giving Anna a few dummy runs. She was also taken on a tour of American television newsrooms to see how the two-handed style of presentation worked over there. Her first outing was to be presenting ITN's *News at One*, in March. Anna admitted afterwards, 'I was a bit nervous, but I was determined to enjoy my first ITN appearance, whatever happened. My chief worry was if anything unexpected came up. I didn't know if I would be able to cope with it. But it didn't.' Everything had gone according to plan. In fact, Angela Rippon, her supposed BBC rival, sent her a telegram of congratulation. It said 'Well done. Welcome to the club.' There then followed some reporting and newsreading over the Easter weekend.

The Cambridge rowers experiencing that sinking feeling during the Boat Race.

When Anna officially joined *News at Ten*, Reggie Bosanquet welcomed her to the programme with a bottle of red wine and two glasses on her new desk. He told her he didn't like women reading the news, though later they did become friends. They would sometimes play darts together in the office before the programme.

Her first appearance on *News at Ten* itself came in April and coincided with something of a revamp for the programme. Out went the old brown desk – in came olive green – and the two presenters were to sit closer together. On Anna's first night Alastair was sitting alongside her. Her popularity with viewers appeared to have some effect on the names they gave their children. Before she got the *News at Ten* job, the

name 'Anna' didn't appear in the list of most popular girls' names in 1978. Two years later, it was the third most popular.

Sandy Gall and Reggie Bosanquet still figured prominently in the new look but Alastair Burnet was

Alastair Burnet and Anna Ford say 'goodnight' as another *News at Ten* comes to an end.

Anna Ford was the new face on *News at Ten*. She quickly struck up an on-screen chemistry with Reginald Bosanquet.

to be the first among equals. The plan was that he would appear four out of five nights one week and, in the following week, three nights out of five. Anna was to do three nights every week. Incidentally, there were some musical chairs on the other ITN programmes. Leonard Parkin was to become the main presenter of *The News at 5.45*. Leonard's place on *News at One* was to be taken by Peter Sissons who was a familiar face to all ITN viewers as its industrial correspondent.

Most people who work on *News at Ten* have their own favourite 'And Finally' stories. Just about everyone knows the one about Reggie and the cat, even if they weren't born in 1978. It is one that didn't have a happy ending for either newscaster or pet. One of the running news stories of the winter had been the firemen's strike. The army were called in with their now famous Green Goddess fire trucks

Micky Doyle, Michael Nicholson and Tom Phillips safe at last after their ordeal in the jungle.

Jungle diet

During the time the crew were missing in the jungle they had no proper food. They had to live on baked caterpillar, roasted grasshopper and maize gruel. Eating was a real problem not just because of the lack of food but because of the flies. They were in cattle country and the sky was black with flies. The cattle had all been slaughtered but the flies still remained. Michael says, 'The only way you could eat was to pull a sleeping bag over your head, put your food inside the bag and eat in complete darkness … otherwise you were eating mouthfuls of flies.'

But there were some meals he enjoyed. Most of the time they ate a kind of porridge made out of maize so anything new was a bonus. 'When I was first offered the caterpillars I thought they were cashew nuts. They had been cooked over a fire and were dark brown and crunchy. Delicious, in fact.'

– ancient vehicles even then and part-built from wood. Not all 'And Finally's have to end with a belly laugh. The report in question certainly didn't. One Green Goddess crew had been called to that most clichéd of rescues – a cat stuck up a tree. The elderly woman who owned it begged the troops to get it down. She was so pleased when they did that she invited them in for tea and biscuits to show her gratitude. Sadly for all concerned, as the heroes set off back towards their barracks, they accidentally ran over the cat and killed it. An unhappy end to the story perhaps – but what really upset the hundreds of viewers who rang into complain was the smirk on Reggie's face as the camera cut back to him at the end of the item. His popularity with Britain's cat lovers took a terrible dive.

Far more serious was the rescue of a *News at Ten* crew who disappeared in Angola. Michael Nicholson, who was by then South Africa correspondent, cameraman Tom Phillips and sound recordist Micky Doyle had gone there on what they thought would be a ten-day trip. Their assignment was to report on the activities of the South African-backed UNITA rebels – led by Dr Jonas Savimbi – in their civil war against the troops of the communist government of Angola which was backed by both Russian and Cuban

forces. It ended up lasting exactly a hundred days longer than they expected.

Three days after arriving in Angola, the lorry in which the ITN team was travelling was fired on by troops supporting the government. It was hit seventeen times. Two of the UNITA troops they were travelling with were wounded. That ambush coincided with the start of an offensive by the pro-government forces against UNITA. The ITN crew were trapped by the fighting – they couldn't move without the help of the UNITA forces. They could not survive in the bush by themselves. In the end, the only way for them to get out was to walk with their UNITA escorts to Dr Savimbi's headquarters in the south of Angola.

The trek of around 1,500 miles through the bush took them seven and a half weeks. Their route couldn't even be in a straight line because they had to make sure they didn't walk into enemy strongholds. They

Prince Michael of Kent caused a stir in May by announcing his engagement to Baroness Marie-Christine von Reibnitz, a Roman Catholic divorcee.

had to cope with scorpions, snakes, plagues of flies, intense heat and the physical punishment and mental monotony of marching for up to twelve hours a day. It was a terrible ordeal – especially for Micky Doyle who suffered terrible damage to his feet and collapsed during the march. The outside world knew nothing of their disappearance: ITN kept it quiet for fear of placing its men in yet more danger. ITN was getting increasingly worried about them and at one stage had four charter planes standing by at different airstrips while attempts were made to establish contact with the missing men. That prompted the wry observation that ITN at that point had the third biggest airforce in southern Africa.

The rescue itself finally came when one of those planes managed to fly in and collect them from Dr Savimbi's headquarters. At first, the UNITA soldiers they were with thought they were coming under attack from pro-government forces – even though a UNITA guide was involved in co-ordinating the rescue. The ITN men waved and shouted, 'It's ours,' as the plane flew into view to stop their escorts from shooting it down. From there, it was homeward bound for the crew.

And Finally...

Magistrates in Hertfordshire ruled that an Alsatian bitch kept at a garage was a guard-dog and fined the owners for failing to have a handler or display a warning notice.

The bemused owners claimed the dog was ten years old, had no teeth, was known affectionately as 'Gums' and also suffered from arthritis.

1979

THE YEAR BEGAN with what became known as the winter of discontent. Unofficial strikes broke out across the country over the Labour government's decision to limit pay rises for public sector workers to five per cent. Rubbish was piling up on street corners and in parks. There were even reports that grave diggers were striking. It was against this that Prime Minister James Callaghan was trying to stay in office. The crunch for him came in March when he faced a no-confidence vote. It was going to be a big night for *News at Ten* whatever happened, with a vote around 10.00pm. Hours of planning had been done to cover every eventuality. Or rather every eventuality but one. Mr Callaghan lost the knife-edge vote. The eventuality that hadn't been covered was that ITN's political editor, Julian Haviland, didn't turn up to do his live report on time. It meant a few changes to the order of the reports on that night's big story.

Unions at ITN had been worrying about pay, like the rest of the country. Like all regular ITV programmes on the network, *News at Ten* was off air for nearly three months in a pay dispute. The first ITN programme back on air after the strike – the *News at 5.45* – began with these words from Leonard Parkin: 'Good evening. It's nice to be back. Now let's get on with it.'

Like many other working environments, ITN has always had office romances – perhaps more than most places. Long hours, uncertain days off and

The Conservative MP Airey Neave, a friend of Prime Minister Margaret Thatcher, was killed by a car bomb as he drove out of the underground car park at the House of Commons. It was planted by the Irish National Liberation Army. Airey Neave was a front-bench spokesman on Northern Ireland.

working under pressure does throw people together. In those early days of a relationship couples often worry that their private lives might somehow compromise their working lives. In June, one rather high-profile office romance became public. Anna Ford and reporter Jon Snow announced they were getting engaged. Anna spoke at the time about how they'd tried to keep it secret: 'We never spoke to each other in the office and we always left separately. When we went out together it was always to country pubs and places where we would not be recognized.' Indeed, their announce-

make his cover story look more convincing. Unfortunately the ploy didn't work first time and he was sent packing on the first plane out – to Athens. Undeterred, he tried the same tactic again a week later. This time it *did* work and he reported the story of the hostage crisis for the next month. Only when he got safely back to London did he hear that the Islamic government had decided all dealers in Persian carpets were being arrested and executed for profiteering at the expense of the state.

By the end of the year, Reggie Bosanquet and *News at Ten* parted company. The announcement came out of the blue. He said it was by mutual consent and there had been no row. Not so much a resignation, he said, as a parting of the ways and ITN went to some lengths to insist he hadn't been sacked – but

Jon Snow and Anna Ford got engaged, but it only lasted four months.

Anna Ford and Sandy Gall checking through their scripts in the newsroom before the start of the programme.

ment surprised some of their colleagues. Anna, by then thirty-five, and Jon, then thirty-one, seemed the perfect television couple. They had more than just their work in common – both had fathers who were clergymen. But it wasn't to be. Four months later, the couple announced the wedding was off. Anna was also in the news for another reason: she was named newscaster of the year.

One of the big stories of the year was Iran. After the Shah had been toppled, Ayatollah Khomeini returned from exile to run the country. Then came the kidnapping of American hostages from the US embassy. John Suchet was sent to cover the story for *News at Ten*. Under the Ayatollah's new Islamic rules, all journalists had been banned from the country. So to try to get in, John had another passport made up which described him as an international carpet salesman – he had business cards printed too to

John Suchet reporting from the streets of Tehran (top), having used a fake business card (above) to get into Iran.

problems had been simmering for some time. Once or twice he just hadn't turned up for work. One story about him illustrates that occasionally he could be awkward. One night Reggie took issue with something going on in the programme. There were just a few minutes to go before transmission. Reggie couldn't be mollified, got up and said, 'That's it, I'm leaving.' He left the studio and went up to the newsroom. He took his coat off the peg and looked to check that everyone could see. In fact the newsroom was practically empty because most people were in the production control room. He walked past the office of one busy executive who was engrossed in something else. 'Cheerio,' said Reggie pointedly, 'I'm off.' The executive, who'd lost track of time and

assumed *News at Ten* was over and had passed off without incident, said, 'Cheerio Reggie, great show, great show.' It was at that point that Reggie realized his protest about whatever it was had been rather futile and he returned to the studio – just in time.

Reggie – now forty-seven – had of course been with *News at Ten* since it started and with ITN for over twenty years. After the dust had settled, he said he'd left because reading *News at Ten* had become like a treadmill and he wanted to get off the programme and do other things.

The Soviet Union invaded Afghanistan at the end of the year. A unit of Soviet special forces seized the airport at the capital, Kabul, on Christmas Eve. This opened up the way for a massive airlift of troops and equipment. Simultaneously, Soviet motorized rifle divisions rumbled across the border.

When news first came through of the invasion, Jon Snow was in Iran, covering the American hostage crisis. Straightaway he headed for the border with Afghanistan. He was there within a few hours. He

Reginald Bosanquet was a keen tennis player who arranged regular matches with his newsroom colleagues.

Inside the *News at Ten* control room.

came across a German-speaking Afghan dental student who agreed to take him into eastern Afghanistan, where he spent a week covering resistance to the invasion and the assault on the Soviet convoys. There was one particularly harrowing occasion. Through his binoculars he could see very young Afghan recruits dowsing themselves in petrol and then clambering on to the turrets of passing Soviet tanks and setting themselves alight.

ITN cameras were to alter out of all recognition thanks to new technology. Film had been the only way of capturing moving images from the beginning of television news. Film meant lengthy chemical processes to develop the negative roll from the camera into pictures that could be manually spliced together for broadcast reports.

Video tape was becoming more common during the late seventies for recording or editing existing pictures but only on huge video tape machines and certainly not in cameras.

Then came ENG – Electronic News Gathering. Basically it was an all-electronic portable camera that used large video tapes instead of film cans. The implications for gathering television news were immense. No longer did reporters or producers on *News at Ten* have to wait for the film to go through the chemical 'bath'. The new ENG tape could be taken straight out of the camera, and immediately edited electronically. ENG also had major industrial relations implications. It meant fewer people were needed to produce the finished product and meant changes in working practices too. The unions, which were still powerful in ITN at the time, didn't like the way it was introduced.

Margaret Thatcher won the 1979 general election to become Britain's first woman Prime Minister.

Perhaps the first time it was used was during coverage of the end of the fighting in Rhodesia – soon to become Zimbabwe. The ITN cameraman sent to Rhodesia was using colour film. The Rhodesia–Zimbabwe Television Corporation could then transmit recorded pictures only in black and white. So an ingenious scheme was developed where the colour film would be played from a projector through a prism and that image could be filmed on the ENG camera by picture editor Peter Read. Once the colour pictures were on the video tape inside the new electronic camera, they could be transmitted back to London, in colour. For the plan to work, the film projector, the prism and the ENG camera had to be lined up in a particular way. Peter was shown how to do this and marks were left on the desk so that everything could be returned to the right place for the next time. A cleaning lady in the television station had other ideas. The next morning, when Peter came to use the same set-up, the marks had been wiped away.

And Finally...

A pet shop in Didcot, Oxfordshire, looked an easy target when burglars broke into it one night. But the premises already had its own security guard. Not a guard dog but an attack rabbit.

Although a woman can handle it completely safely, the harmless-looking creature had a burning and vicious hatred for men and would sink teeth or claws into any male body that came within range, and had actually put a man in hospital.

The unusual guardian was kept locked up during the day for the protection of any male customers that might come in, but at night it was led out to roam freely, ready to deal with any male intruders.

1980

NEWS AT TEN went to cover the Zimbabwean elections, with a plan to go live on election night. Nothing like it had ever been done before. Alastair Burnet and a colour camera were flown out from ITN but most of the technicians and all of the technology were supplied by the Zimbabweans – or rather by white army officers on what amounted to national service.

On the night before the results were due, an ITN reporter had got some early returns from outlying areas which, unlike the polls, suggested that Robert Mugabe was going to win and not the caretaker Prime Minister Bishop Abel Muzorewa – the candidate favoured by the whites. *News at Ten* therefore went live the night before the result was due, saying that Mugabe was going to win. The white technicians, in their uniforms, froze in horror as Alastair spoke the words. However, it turned out Mr Mugabe did win, as Alastair was able to confirm the following night.

The next day Alastair and *News at Ten* colleagues Sue Tinson and Diana Edwards-Jones went sightseeing at Victoria Falls before flying home. Lots of black people kept coming up to Alastair because they heard he had correctly predicted the election result. They shook his hand and said, 'Thank you for giving us back our freedom.'

ITN's twenty-fifth anniversary was marked by a visit from the Queen and the Duke of Edinburgh. On

The Queen's visit to the *News at Ten* studio.

duty on *News at Ten* that night were Alastair and Anna Ford. Anna had to explain to the Queen that she couldn't get up to talk to her because she was already wired up with her earpiece, ready for that night's programme. If she had stood up as normal etiquette might require, the sticky tape that secures the wires to the back of her dress – out of sight of the viewers – might have come undone. That night Alastair was in the number one chair, but Anna – now a veteran of two years – got her chance in February. Sitting alongside her in her more usual seat was ITN's then diplomatic editor, Michael Brunson.

ITN's coverage of the ending of the Iranian Embassy siege is still talked about in newsroom corridors and nearby pubs.

The siege began when terrorists took over the embassy in Knightsbridge in West London. For six days they tried to extract promises from officials in the embassy that political prisoners in Iran would be released. The stand-off came to an end when they shot one of the embassy's press attachés and threatened to shoot another hostage every thirty minutes. ITN broke into the ITV schedule at 7.27pm to broadcast live the dramatic moment after the SAS stepped in. It was to become known as ITN's longest newsflash – ITN was on the air for forty minutes.

It didn't get off to the best of starts, though. Anna Ford couldn't be found to read the newsflash so reporter Jeremy Hands was sent into a sound booth to go on air – though out of vision. He started the commentary and then handed over to Anthony Carthew at the scene who kept up the commentary on the extraordinary pictures that were to follow.

ITN's coverage outshone that of the BBC because of an ITN camera which, unknown to other media, had been smuggled round the back of the building. Everyone else's cameras were round the front. The ITN camera showed the masked SAS men abseiling from the roof, breaking in through the picture windows as strategically positioned explosives were detonated. From inside the building came the sound of gunshots as the Iranian terrorists shot dead one of their hostages and wounded another. The dramatic action lasted for eleven minutes from beginning to end and was one of the most memorable sequences of live news pictures. The newsflash got its own mention in that week's viewing figures – eleven million people had watched it. It won critical acclaim too with a Royal Television Society Award.

There were slightly different problems facing the production team for that night's *News at Ten*, caused by the very camera that, earlier in the evening, had brought such memorable pictures. Because the ITN camera wasn't linked into the main outside broadcast unit, it wasn't 'synchronous' which means

The SAS ending the siege of the Iranian Embassy in London. An ITN camera located at the rear of the building captured the dramatic conclusion. The pictures ITN got from this hidden camera gained them eleven million viewers and a Royal Television Society Award.

in simple terms it wasn't quite on the same wavelength as the other two cameras. When the video tape recording of the storming of the embassy was played back there were large chunks where the images were rolling about in the frame and were therefore unsuitable for editing. In the end, there were just enough useable pictures for that night's dramatic programme.

ITN kept pretty quiet afterwards about how that camera had got round the back of the embassy. In fact it was smuggled into a flat. At the time, all they would say was that it had been put in place on the final day. It was, by any standards, very good timing.

Iran's war with its neighbour Iraq created another rescue situation involving a *News at Ten* reporter – this time Jon Snow. Rescues in war-torn areas might be considered part and parcel of the job of a *News at Ten* foreign correspondent – but reporting them, not actually co-ordinating them. But that was the role thrust on to Jon Snow as he reported the Iran–Iraq war. A British cargo ship – the *Altanin* – had been trapped in the fighting for six weeks in the Shatt al Arab waterway, between Iran and Iraq. On board were British sailors and their wives and Filipino crewmen. The British owner of the boat had been ringing the Foreign Office for weeks asking them for help in getting the boat freed. The Foreign Office apparently told him that it wasn't in the waterway and must have moved on. Then one night the boat's owner was watching *News at Ten* at home when he saw the *Altanin* over Jon's shoulder in his report. He rang ITN to ask if there was anything Jon could do. In return he offered to make Jon the ship's agent, which would give him access to Basra dockyard – normally off-limits to journalists.

With help from the *Altanin*'s owner back in London, Jon was able to contact a Norwegian ship in the area which was in coded radio contact once a day with the *Altanin*. Jon was able to discover there was a total of fifty-six people on board. They had welded down the

Jon Snow reporting from Afghanistan.

hatches of the ship – a bulk ore carrier – and were hiding below decks. Any rescue attempt had to be kept secret. A similar attempt involving a different ship had ended in the deaths of five crewmen. Jon and his Iraqi contact – a commando – put on wet suits and flippers and swam out to the ship at low tide. The only problem was that in agreeing a time, Jon hadn't realized the captain on board was working to GMT not local time so the swim began three hours after low tide. In the swirling currents of the incoming tide Jon and the Iraqi commando were nearly swept into the line of Iranian fire. When they did get on board they eventually agreed to give a signal the following night for the *Altanin* to lower its lifeboats and get the people off. It was one of the first times the new electronic cameras – with their superior night-time capabilities – had been used on a foreign assignment. Had it been a film camera, *News at Ten* viewers would never have seen the pictures of the people clambering off the ship. Jon Snow's coverage of that story and reports from Afghanistan won him the award for television reporter of the year.

Jon covered another big foreign story that year: the war in El Salvador. Jon and his crew were sent there after the assassination of Archbishop Oscar Arnulfo Romero – a people's champion who had spoken out

Anna Ford

Anna Ford was brought up in Wigton in Cumbria, and went to Manchester University where she studied economics and social anthropology and was President of the Students' Union. She became a staff tutor with the Open University and then joined Granada Television in Manchester as a researcher. She became a reporter on their local evening news programme, *Granada Reports*.

She then moved to the BBC to work on *Man Alive*, before joining *Tomorrow's World* as its main presenter and successor to Raymond Baxter. In 1978 Anna Ford became the first woman to present *News at Ten* and was one of its regular newscasters until 1981.

She was one of the 'Famous Five' who launched *TV-am* that year, and later hit the headlines by throwing wine over Jonathan Aitken, then chief executive of *TV-am* who had sacked her and her colleagues from the breakfast station.

Anna has been a presenter of BBC1's *Six O'Clock News* since 1989 and of Radio 4's *Today* programme since 1993.

Alastair Burnet and Sandy Gall, the senior *News at Ten* newscasters in the 1980s.

against both left and right wing extremists in El Salvador. Unlike in Afghanistan or Poland, any journalist could get into El Salvador. As Jon admits, 'Before I went, I didn't know if it had an Atlantic or Pacific coast'. When Jon arrived, his was the first foreign television crew to start covering the story. Suddenly, his reports were alerting the world to what was going on there. He sent thirty-nine reports back to London in forty-two days.

'What we found,' he said, 'was a country that had staggered straight out of the pages of a Graham Greene novel – white stuccoed buildings, and churches with coffins lined up outside.' It was a

terrible war but it was one which suited the demands of television – and not just for the beautiful backdrop. It is a country roughly the size of Wales. That meant Jon and his crew could cross the front line two or three times a day and still get back to their base and file their report on the same day.

One particular day tragically illustrated that point. In the morning they had been filming with one group of guerrillas in a village. In the afternoon they crossed the front line and went with the army whose soldiers opened fire on the same village – killing the people they had been with in the morning.

Another *News at Ten* stalwart known for his action-man reporting is Sandy Gall – so it's not too surprising that he helped organize a challenging

Anna Ford and Sandy Gall at work in the newsroom.

charity walk in the Cairngorms that summer in his capacity as rector of Aberdeen University. What was more surprising was that he persuaded his colleagues, Anna Ford and Alastair Burnet, to join him. In the end it was Anna who was the first to finish the twenty-mile trek in a creditable six hours. She had done some training – a ten-mile hike the weekend before. Sandy said he'd been jogging in his climbing boots by way of preparation. Alastair's concession to getting fit was to use the stairs at work instead of the lift. The sight of them striking out across the Lairig Ghru Pass was remarkable for one other reason. Also in the party was a young Grampian television presenter called Selina Scott.

And Finally...

Tuam Golf Club near Galway, west of Ireland, was plagued by a bizarre thief. More and more golfers were losing their balls, not to hazards or the rough but to a fast-moving filcher in the shape of a crow.

The bird had apparently acquired a taste for golf balls, swooping down at every opportunity and flapping away with its prize which it then dropped into a nearby bog. On one memorable day it was said to have taken more than twenty off the fairway.

On one occasion, the airborne raider dived on two unsuspecting golfers, who had both just reached the green only to see the crow make off with both their balls!

1981

THE LONG-AWAITED NEWS that Prince Charles was to marry Lady Diana Spencer came in February. The speculation had been almost running out of control. Carol Barnes was the reporter assigned to the story of the Royal Romance – a story that had some parallels with what was going on in her own life at the time.

Before the announcement came, Carol and her crew had been waiting outside Lady Di's flat in Kensington in West London for hours. Her soundman on that occasion was Nigel Thomson. Eventually Diana came out and Carol pushed through the other reporters to talk to her. As the throng pursued Diana along the pavement, Nigel was walking backwards holding his microphone towards Diana who straightaway told him to watch out or else he would crash into a lamp post behind him. Carol's own romance with Nigel started soon after that.

The parallels though didn't end there. Carol – who was one of the reporters on the day of the Royal Wedding – married Nigel in Camden Register Office the next day. The following year Diana was pregnant with Prince William at the same time as Carol was pregnant with her son James. James arrived first. Diana, it seems, read about Carol's happy news in the papers and sent her a telegram saying, 'From one lady-in-waiting to another – Congratulations.'

The clamour for union recognition in Poland had begun in its shipyards. The growth and spread of the

Carol Barnes was assigned to cover the story of Lady Diana Spencer's romance with Prince Charles.

Solidarity union met first with embarrassment and then with force from Poland's communist leaders. They tried to stop foreign journalists from getting to the shipyards at Gdansk and Szczecin. When John Suchet was sent to cover the story for *News at Ten* he found he could get in by taking a ferry from Sweden and obtaining a tourist visa on the boat – no questions asked. John and his crew went to Szczecin, got caught filming and were arrested. They were taken to the local police headquarters for questioning, persuaded the police they were tourists and were released.

They next day they tried to do more secret filming at Szczecin and were arrested again. They were taken to the same interrogation room but with a different

The Brixton riots by night (above) and the aftermath (above right). Hundreds of people turned the streets of south London into a battlefield in April as they went on a rampage of looting, vandalism and arson.

interrogator. John was just on the point of convincing the policeman that they were tourists when another one came in and whispered in the first policeman's ear. He looked up and said, 'You were in this room yesterday,' and John and the crew were put on the next plane out.

Anna Ford announced she was leaving ITN and read her last *News at Ten* in March. Her decision mirrored that of her BBC rival Angela Rippon who was also leaving the BBC. Together they were going to join David Frost and Peter Jay on the new ITV breakfast television station, *TV-am*.

Once again, the hunt was on for a glamorous new presenter to partner the venerable men of *News at Ten*. It didn't take long to find Anna's successor. It was to be Selina Scott – then twenty-nine – the presenter of Grampian Television's local evening news programme *North Tonight*. It was said she was in line to get Angela Rippon's job at the BBC before ITN got in first – offering her £25,000 a year. The negotiations were made all the more difficult because she was moving house at the time and didn't have a telephone in the flat where she was living. Phone

conversations with Wells Street were carried out in her office in the newsroom at Grampian Television in Aberdeen. Despite saying she was superstitious, she signed her contract on Friday 13 February. She said at the time, 'I think you can make your own luck sometimes.' Of her new job she said, 'I seem to be very fortunate. After all, I didn't apply for it. I don't expect to be on *News at Ten* straight away. I shall be easing myself in slowly.' In fact she made her *News at Ten* debut in May – once again it was Alastair Burnet who partnered the latest new girl.

Selina was to play a key role in the biggest story of the year, the Royal Wedding. She was joined in an early morning scene-setter for the day ahead by the former *News at Ten* man Andrew Gardner – as ITN and Andrew's new employers, Thames Television, pooled their resources for a total of nine hours of programming. Alastair Burnet provided the commentary for the service. ITV viewers saw wonderful views of the scenes of celebration, from a live camera mounted on the Goodyear airship. The night before the big day, hundreds of people had gathered in Hyde Park for a celebratory firework display which was supposed to start at ten o'clock, but was actually a few minutes late. That was because *News at Ten* wanted to show it live and didn't want to miss the dramatic opening. A certain amount of gentle persuasion was then applied to the man in charge of the display. The argument went

Selina Scott

Selina Scott started her television career at Grampian Television, as a presenter and reporter. She was headhunted by ITN and became one of the regular newscasters of *News at Ten* in May 1981, working alongside Alastair Burnet and Sandy Gall. Although she was a presenter of the programme for just a year and a half she quickly rose to stardom and has remained an international celebrity ever since.

When she left the programme in 1982 she launched BBC's *Breakfast Time* and went on to present the UK's first fashion magazine programme, the BBC's *Clothes Show*.

She presented a series of documentaries on the royal heads of Europe, including profiles of Prince Charles and King Juan Carlos of Spain.

In 1986 Selina Scott worked for American network television on the current affairs magazine programme *West 57*. In 1995 she had her own talk show for NBC Superchannel in Europe, produced by ITN in the UK. From 1996 to 1997 Selina presented London Weekend Television's crime prevention show, *Eye Spy*.

ITN cameras covered what then seemed to be the fairytale marriage of the Prince of Wales and Lady Diana Spencer at St Paul's Cathedral in July.

that if he delayed its start by a few minutes, it would be seen by millions of people around the country as well as the hundreds in the park. The man very kindly agreed.

So the fireworks were cued by the *News at Ten* control room. The production assistant told the floor manager at the park when to ask the pyrotechnic experts to light the blue touch paper. That was how *News at Ten* showed the precise moment when the

sky over Hyde Park erupted so dramatically into colour and light.

One of the other main stories of the summer – a world away from fairytale weddings – was the inner city riots in London, Liverpool and Manchester. Television news coverage of the disturbances itself came under attack for encouraging copycat violence. It was a charge *News at Ten* staunchly refuted.

Peter Sharp was appointed ITN's Southern Africa correspondent and decided he should learn to speak Afrikaans – the language of the white government. When he was working on the road, he would often be staying in hotels and would pick up the phone whenever he wanted anything. The operator would say good morning, or at least that is what Peter thought they were saying. The next time he met the South African Foreign Minister, Pik Botha, he decided to try out the new greeting. '*Goeie more Skaakelbor,*' said Peter to Mr Botha, whereupon Mr Botha and his officials fell about laughing. What Peter had actually said was 'Good morning, Switchboard.'

And Finally...

A man appeared in court in Stornoway in the Outer Hebrides, charged with stealing the ignition key of a truck... by swallowing it.

The culprit and two friends were said to be 'well-oiled' when the incident happened.

Determined to prove their case, the police did an X-ray of the man's stomach before nature could take its course. However, their efficiency was their undoing when the sheriff refused to accept the pictorial evidence. According to him, the police should have obtained a search warrant first.

1982

THERE CAN BE NO DOUBT what the biggest story of the year was. Britain ended up going to war against Argentina over a group of islands few people had ever heard of. In the early stages of the Falklands crisis Mrs Thatcher gave an interview to *News at Ten*. Argentinian forces had captured the islands in the South Atlantic, seizing the islands' capital Port Stanley after overwhelming the company of Royal Marines stationed there. Asked if she would resign if she failed to reclaim the Falklands, she famously replied, 'Failure? The possibility does not exist.'

Two aircraft carriers – HMS *Hermes* and HMS *Invincible* – set off from Portsmouth at the start of April for the Falklands 8,000 miles away. ITN camera teams were on the HMS *Hermes*. It was an emotional day – and a day of uncertainty too. At that time, no one knew whether there would *be* a war. Ministry of Defence officials did allow ITN to put a satellite dish on one of its ships only because they had been told by their experts that it wouldn't be possible to transmit from it. The military radar signals would block any transmission. They hadn't reckoned on ITN engineer Peter Heaps. By the time the dish reached Ascension Island he had worked out a way of sending some form of live pictures. The MoD was so staggered at what he'd managed to do that he was asked to leave the ship – with all his gear – at Ascension Island. There was also the small problem that his transmissions were interfering with military radar and communication signals.

The Princess of Wales meeting Sandy Gall and Selina Scott in the ITN newsroom.

The task force – numbering forty ships – sailed as the frantic diplomatic activity continued. There were worries in Whitehall about trying to conduct a war so far from home but Mrs Thatcher felt the Argentinian invasion left her no choice but to respond with force. Royal Marine commandos recaptured the island of South Georgia which the Argentinians had taken three weeks earlier. The ITN news that night was watched by seventeen million people. It showed Mrs Thatcher standing in Downing Street – with Defence Secretary John Nott – saying, 'Let us congratulate our armed forces and the Marines. Rejoice. Rejoice.' The story was to change for the worse after that.

At the start of May, the submarine HMS *Conqueror* sank the Argentinian cruiser, *General Belgrano*. Two days later HMS *Sheffield* was destroyed by an Argentinian Exocet missile. It was the first British warship to be sunk since the Second World War. A fortnight after that HMS *Coventry* and a container ship – the *Atlantic Conveyor*, which was taking supplies for the troops – were both hit. Two further warships, HMS *Ardent* and HMS *Antelope*, were sunk at the end of the month. British Marine commandos were by now 'yomping' across the island – eventually recapturing the village of Goose Green after a battle in which Colonel 'H' Jones – the commander of the 2nd Parachute Regiment – was killed. Two of the British landing ships, *Sir Galahad* and *Sir Tristram*, were hit at the start of June. By the middle of June British troops had recaptured the island. The British losses in the Falklands war were put at 255. The Argentinians had lost 652.

The frightening and terrible events of the war had unfolded in the homes of millions of people. However, there was often a delay of several days in those reports reaching the screens – and not just because of the immense logistical problems caused by the huge distances involved. The Ministry of Defence didn't want sensitive information being inadvertently broadcast and insisted on censoring the reports. So the news of the latest developments

Mrs Thatcher telling Britain to rejoice that the Royal Marines had recaptured the island of South Georgia in the Falklands.

Britain fighting for the Falklands. British troops 'yomp' towards final victory at Port Stanley (top). A vigilant gunner on standby in case of an early morning Argentinian attack (above).

were often read out by a civil servant in the Ministry of Defence at a regular daily press conference – before viewers were able to see the pictures. Ian McDonald became a household name for *News at Ten* viewers for the six weeks that the war lasted.

ITN's editor David Nicholas had wanted to get round the censorship by trying to charter an oil tanker – in collaboration with the American Network ABC. He wanted to sail it to the Falklands with a satellite dish on board. He abandoned the idea only when Lloyd's of London told him it would not be possible to insure it. David was also instrumental in a very important area of policy. *News at Ten* would not broadcast news agency reports of British ships being hit by Argentinian missiles. Only if the information came from the Ministry of Defence would it appear on *News at Ten*. David didn't want families of servicemen hearing unsubstantiated reports that might not be true. He was proved right when one report said HMS *Sheffield* had been sunk with all lives lost when in fact some survived.

Military censorship wasn't the only issue raised by the television news coverage of the war. There was also the issue of impartiality of reporting. ITN felt that the war should be reported from a British perspective – though not of course in a jingoistic way – when British lives were being lost in a war with a foreign enemy. They were issues that would continue to be debated long after the war was over. But those arguments were put to one side as the task force of ships sailed back to their home ports to scenes of great rejoicing and relief for those who had survived.

There was rejoicing too for Britain's Roman Catholics when John Paul II become the first Pope for 450 years to come here. Usually Thames Television mounted special outside broadcasts to cover events of national importance, but this time ITN was to play the lead role. After months of planning, there were worries at ITN that the Falklands War might put paid to his visit. It was scheduled to take place while the war was going on. Alastair Stewart was sent to Rome with *News at Ten* programme editor Stewart Purvis who was later to become ITN's editor-in-chief and chief executive. Their assignment was to find out whether the Pope would still come.

One day there was a papal mass. Alastair had gone back to the local television station to file a report. Stewart stayed at the mass with an Italian cameraman and was able to ask the Pope, during a walkabout at the end of the mass, whether he would still come to Britain. 'Yes,' said the Pope, 'I will.' That was quite a story. The only problem was, as the Pope spoke to Stewart, his cameraman bent down to kiss the Pope's hand so while His Holiness's words were heard, viewers had only a glimpse of his face.

The ITN teams in the Falklands weren't the only ones in danger that year. Reporter Desmond Hamill, cameraman Sebastian Rich, sound recordist Nigel Thomson and picture editor Peter Read were kidnapped in the Lebanon by Kurdish militiamen. They

Comedy duo Morecambe and Wise picked up a few tips from *News at Ten* duo Gall and Scott (above and opposite).

demanded a ransom and made it quite clear the television team would be killed if the money wasn't paid. During an Israeli attack on the outskirts of Beirut in June, a taxi carrying Desmond and his crew was hit by a shell. Their Kurdish driver was killed. The dead man's family appeared to have blamed the ITN men for what happened. The family contacted a group of armed Kurds in the city, and shortly afterwards the kidnap took place. ITN paid £20,000 – and the men were freed unharmed.

In October Selina Scott announced she was leaving *News at Ten* after just eighteen months. In that short time she had established herself as one of television's best-known faces. She had also attracted the unwanted attention of a stalker – which ended up with a court order banning the man from contacting her or ITN. Her last programme was at the end of November. She, like Anna before her, was going to breakfast television. For Selina, it was the new BBC television programme, sitting alongside Frank Bough

on the early morning sofa. Nonetheless, Selina was slightly surprised when Alastair Burnet, presenting alongside her that night, said the next time the viewers would see her would be 'at breakfast time on another channel'.

Would ITN once again try to find a female replacement? No, was the immediate answer. ITN decided it need look only as far as its own Martyn Lewis – who was confirmed as a regular member of the *News at Ten* team.

And Finally...

The destroyer HMS *Bristol* was patrolling five miles off the Falkland Islands when it received a direct hit from an unexpected flying object. To the surprise of the crew a king cormorant had flown into the ship's radar array.

The crew cared for the rather battered bird and christened it Bo Bo. The bird stayed with the ship when it returned to the UK, and Bo Bo took up permanent residence in the safer precincts of London Zoo.

The attack on *Sir Galahad* & *Sir Tristram*, 9 June 1982

The attack happened so fast there wasn't even time to think of finding cover and as ships were hit, men on board didn't have time to put on their anti-burn asbestos head masks and gloves to save them from the heat. As the bombs exploded many were brought ashore with burns.

The two landing ships, *Sir Galahad* and *Sir Tristram*, were bombed 200 yards from each other in a narrow estuary at Fitzroy. The men had come to join other troops which have established positions from here only seven miles from Stanley.

Sir Galahad had anchored only a few hours before and the men were waiting for landing craft to come and get them off. One hour later and most of the men would have been safely ashore in their trenches.

Our air defences, which had come off the ships that morning, were still being set up on the hillside overlooking the estuary. Had the Argentine planes come just that hour later they would have been ready for them. As it was the Skyhawks came in, attacked and were out again with our gunfire chasing them too late. The bombs hit *Sir Galahad* aft, through the engine room and the accommodation section. I watched from the shore less than 400 yards away. The impact made boxes of ammunition on board explode, shaking the ground beneath us, and the soldiers and ourselves crouched as bullets from the ship whistled and whirled past us. We could see them coming by their red tracers. I saw hundreds of men rush forward along the decks, across the hold, putting on their lifejackets, pulling on survival suits, some ship's crewmen just off watch, pulling on shirts and trousers.

Inflatable rubber liferafts, bright orange, were hurled over the side. Some immediately burst into flames as debris from the explosion hit them. Others landed but were blown by the wind into the burning oil.

The strong wind fanned the flames - enormous flames - as the fuel tank exploded, the ship was half enveloped in black, thick smoke, but the Royal Navy Sea King and Wessex helicopter pilots and their crews ignored the flames. They ignored the explosions and ignored the ammunition exploding around them and flew their machines into the smoke to lift the queues of men waiting calmly below.

Lifeboats were launched from *Sir Tristram* - the other ship who seemed to be containing their fire - and these boats under power began taking some of the liferafts in tow. Pilots in the helicopters waiting at the bow, waiting to bring men aboard them, saw what was happening and immediately four of them took their machines to the rear of the ship by the flames.

They came down low and using the down draught of their rotor blades slowly began to push the rubber dinghies away. There was much heroism at Fitzroy but this single tribute must be paid to the helicopter pilots and their winchmen who saved so many.

Michael Nicholson, *News at Ten*, Bluff Cove

1983

BY MAY IT WAS becoming clear there was to be another face joining the *News at Ten* presenting team. Pamela Armstrong – then thirty-one – was presenting the Channel 4 health programme *Well Being*. A month later Pamela had a screen test but still no announcement. In fact she didn't join until the end of the year when her Channel 4 series had finished.

1983 was election year and ITN pioneered a new approach to covering the party leaders. A specific reporter and crew were to be allocated to each leader. Michael Brunson was to cover Mrs Thatcher, David

Rose was assigned to the Labour leader Michael Foot, and Alastair Stewart reported on the Liberal leader David Steel. They were called 'target teams'. It is a concept that ITN still uses in covering election campaigns and one which has been adopted by other television news organizations since. It was a good system but one which could throw up the occasional logistical hitch.

Pamela Armstrong, in the centre of the picture, being welcomed to the *News at Ten* team by colleagues Leonard Parkin, programme director Diana Edwards-Jones, Alastair Burnet, and programme editor Sue Tinson.

During one day of campaigning Michael Foot was driving along in an open-topped bus. It was a prearranged photo opportunity close to a deadline so the ITN team arranged a very complicated scheme to get the pictures back to London. This involved David Rose – who was on the bus with his cameraman and Mr Foot – throwing the video tape into an ITN car that producer Simon Bucks was to drive alongside. Unfortunately, the theory was better than the practice. Special Branch officers looking after Mr Foot wouldn't let the ITN car alongside. So Simon had to overtake the bus on the inside by driving along the pavement. Simon was stopped by police but he did manage to get the tape in time to feed it back to London.

There was one other tricky moment for the team covering Mr Foot, after they became quite friendly with one of his bodyguards. After a late-night dinner, they all decided they'd like to go for a swim in the pool of the hotel they were staying in. By this time it was about 3.00am. They virtually broke into the pool house and had a swim. Then a sauna seemed like a good idea. When eventually the hotel manager found out what was going on, he found a group of men stark naked, apart from one, the bodyguard, who was still wearing his holster.

On election night itself ITN achieved one of its biggest ever coups. Everyone knew Mrs Thatcher was going to win, so a certain amount of drama that night had to be manufactured. Then came the brilliant idea. During the Pope's visit to Britain a camera had been placed inside his 'Popemobile'. Now because of the advances in satellite technology, it might be possible to put a camera in the back of the car taking Mrs Thatcher from her constituency count in North London to Downing Street and broadcast live pictures. Siren voices said it couldn't be done … and that she wouldn't agree. But engineer Peter Heaps proved it could be done. A small camera could be placed inside the car, facing Mrs Thatcher sitting in the back. The camera cable would go

ITN's election-night scoop. A victorious Margaret Thatcher in her car.

through to the boot, to a transmitter which could send the pictures to an ITN truck that was allowed to join Mrs Thatcher's convoy to Number Ten. The ITN truck would then send the pictures up to a helicopter which could then send them back to ITN's election studios.

Mrs Thatcher's press officers liked the idea and kindly agreed not to tell anyone else about the plan, apart from her of course. She too quite liked the idea but she had one problem with it. How would she know when the pictures from the camera were appearing live on television screens around the country? She wouldn't like the watching millions to be able to see her scratching her nose, for example. No one at ITN much liked the idea of her having a switch to turn it off, in case she forgot to turn it back on again. So a simple solution was thought up. She was given a piece of black velvet that she could place across the lens whenever she wanted to. In fact she never did so. The live pictures, when they appeared, were a triumph. They were the highlight of the night's programme.

During the war in Lebanon the main media hotel was the Commodore in Beirut. Journalists from all over the world stayed there and even in the worst of times they were well looked after. One of the long-term residents

The election-night programme *The Nation Decides* presented by Martyn Lewis, Peter Sissons and Alastair Burnet (opposite). The election studio (above). The team of presenters, and journalists collating the results flooding in from constituencies around the country on the floor below.

of the hotel was a grey parrot named Coco. He became famous during the war because he learned to imitate the sound of incoming shells whistling through the air – his highly realistic impression often giving the unwary a nasty moment. A patriotic Frenchman had succeeded in teaching Coco the first few bars of 'La Marseillaise'. ITN sound recordist Mike Coe had rather different musical taste. Through persistence, kindness and a lot of sunflower seeds he managed to subvert the French national anthem to 'Hey Girl Don't Bother Me' by the Tamms, much to the disgust of the French and the delight of almost everyone else. Coco was eventually kidnapped and killed by Shiite fundamentalist fighters, presumably for having such a good time. The staff at the Commodore were quite

Rocket attack in Beirut.

imperturbable; one night Mike phoned down to the telephone operator in high dudgeon. He had been waiting for an hour for his call and he had paid the requisite ten-dollar bribe to speed things up. The operator explained, in a quiet voice, that there was a gun battle going on in reception and they were all hiding under the front desk.

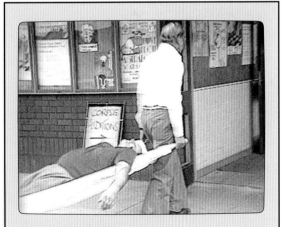

And Finally...

Jobs where the essential requirement is to lie-about all the time are few and far between, but this was exactly what a theatre director was offering when he advertised in Taunton, Somerset. The position – a prone one – was to play the part of a corpse in a Tom Stoppard play.

INTERVIEW
Selina Scott

'I've never worked on a programme quite like *News at Ten*. It had enormous style and verve,' says Selina Scott.

She joined *News at Ten* early in 1981. ITN had been searching for a female newscaster to replace Anna Ford, and had decided it should be twenty-nine-year-old Selina who was then presenting *North Tonight* on Grampian Television in Aberdeen.

The offer was made to her in an unconventional manner: 'I didn't come down to London for an interview,' she recalls. 'ITN sent me a letter asking if I'd meet Alastair Burnet and Diana Edwards-Jones – *News at Ten*'s director – in a remote Aberdeenshire hotel. I remember that night a deep snow had fallen but a huge log fire was burning inside and Alastair and Diana were waiting for me. Diana came straight out with it: "We want you to come to *News at Ten*. There's no question – you've got to do it."'

Selina felt at home from the beginning. 'As a newcomer to ITN, everyone gave me their full backing and confidence. Alastair Burnet was truly professional and was never less than supportive.'

Within weeks of starting *News at Ten*, Selina was co-presenting the coverage of the wedding of the Prince of Wales to Lady Diana Spencer. The night before the ceremony, the presenters were staying in a London hotel. 'Alastair went to his room next door to mine saying he was going to get a good night's sleep and get up early in the morning. But all night long I heard him tapping on the typewriter. He was extremely thorough – nothing got past him.'

Selina says: 'I not only enjoyed my time on *News at Ten*, I learned a lot and it was a very fast learning curve for me. There were many talented people, the support team were excellent and from Alastair I learned how to remain calm, and also to be independent when necessary.' She recalls: 'I was presenting *News at Ten* one night with Alastair. It was during the Falklands War when a piece of paper was put on the desk in front of him. Reports were coming in that a British frigate had gone down with all hands lost. Alastair refused to read

Selina Scott brought a little extra sunshine to the smile of comedian Eric Morecambe when he and partner Ernie Wise visited ITN.

it out on air. It had not been confirmed. As families of servicemen were listening to the news and later it transpired not to be correct – Alastair's instincts had been right all along.'

When the Falklands conflict started Selina had been working on *News at Ten* for a year. She was a household name and had acquired celebrity status. The staff in the ITN postroom were used to the daily influx of fan mail for her, but they were now bringing her post from further afield. Suddenly Selina received a lot of letters from British troops in the Falklands. So ITN very quickly arranged for a special photo to be taken. 'I remember I was wearing a grey jacket and a white shirt looking quite formidable! I signed it, thousands of copies were printed and airlifted out to the troops.' Selina laughs at the memory of becoming 'the forces' sweetheart', saying: 'It was part of ITN's very own war effort.'

Selina shared an office in Wells Street with Sandy Gall, Martyn Lewis and Leonard Parkin. 'There would often be an exotic aroma coming from Sandy's corner where he would be huddled, more often than not, with ex-terrorists and freedom fighters who were swathed in all sorts of unusual garb usually discussing Sandy's next war adventure.'

The ITN newscasters and reporters were not the only famous faces in the building. 'There were always different celebrities coming in. The Princess of Wales visited us in early 1982 when she was expecting William. I remember the two of us got stuck in the ITN lift as I was showing her around. We had an entourage of men behind us but we were so caught up in discussing who my latest boyfriend was that the visit turned into one of the most hilarious I have ever encountered!'

Selina felt ITN's profile was given leverage by David Nicholas who was ITN's editor at the time: 'Few television executives have as much courage as David. He always went the last mile if he believed it right to do so – or was following his instinct for the best news story of the day.'

1984

NEWS AT TEN had the brightest possible start of 1984. The programme's most senior newscaster was made Sir Alastair in the New Year's Honours for services to journalism and broadcasting. He modestly told colleagues when it was announced that it was an award that the whole of the newsroom had a share in. While Alastair always expected to be treated like any other member of the team – no one was ever so familiar with him as to call him 'Al' and certainly not just after his knighthood. But that is just what one junior soundman did when fitting Alastair and Martyn Lewis with their earpieces. 'So, Al,' he said, 'which ear do you want your earpiece in?' Alastair was heard to reply, 'The ear where it won't show when I turn towards my friend Mart.'

Alastair Burnet congratulating an inflatable Ronald Reagan at the Republican convention in New Orleans. Mr Reagan went on to win a second term as President of the USA in a landslide victory against his democratic opponent Walter Mondale.

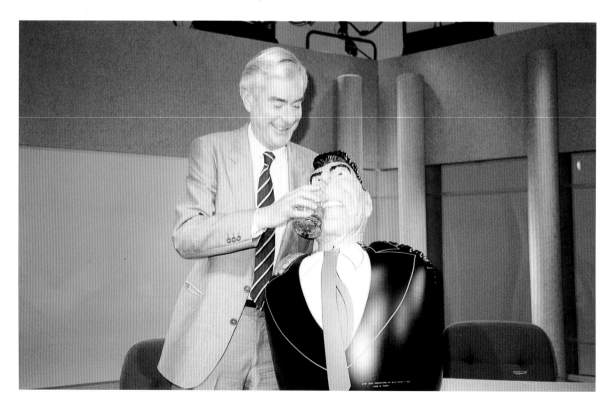

Very sad news, though, about another member of that original team. Reggie Bosanquet died at the age of fifty-one. There was a memorial service for him attended by many of his former colleagues and friends. Andrew Gardner summed up the occasion at the time: 'This is not a solemn service of remembrance – rather it is a celebration of Reggie and an occasion to look back on the fond memories with laughter.'

News at Ten's coverage of the Apollo moon landings of the late sixties and early seventies had won many friends including some at NASA and this helped give *News at Ten* a world exclusive more than a decade later in January. One such friend from NASA came to London to see ITN's science editor at that time, Frank Miles, for lunch at the American's favourite restaurant, The Wig and Pen Club in the Strand. Like many Americans, he enjoyed the historic charm of the Tudor building. Over dinner, the NASA man confided to Frank that within a few

Reggie Bosanquet on set (above) and powdering his nose with television make-up (below).

days, President Reagan would be announcing that America was to build a permanent space station to orbit the earth. 'How do you know?' Frank asked. 'Because,' said the man from NASA, 'the President has asked me to write the section of the speech

Police clashed with striking miners at Orgreave in June.

announcing it, to make sure he gets it right.' He passed a brown NASA envelope under the table. 'In there,' he said, 'you will find drawings of what the space station will look like.' Frank asked if he could use them right away. The American shrugged his shoulders. The next day's *News at Ten* carried the report that President Reagan would shortly be announcing the space station and the programme was able to show what it was going to look like. Sure enough, ten days later, in the exact words of the man from NASA, President Reagan set out the plans for his ambitious project.

The miners' strike began in March – Orgreave coking plant in South Yorkshire was the venue for frightening pitched battles between police, striking miners and their supporters. Mounted police made several charges before order was restored. ITN cameramen had some of the most dramatic pictures of the events.

In a very different setting, one ITN cameraman gave the young Prince William his first look at a television camera – and the one-year-old royal seemed very at home with both it and the microphone. Alan Downes let the Prince look down the viewfinder of his camera during a photo session with the Prince and Princess of Wales.

Technology continued to march on apace with ITN – once again at the forefront – buying the first satellite news-gathering equipment. That meant *News at Ten* could have live reports from almost anywhere in the world it wanted so long as the portable satellite dish could be moved there in time. In the past, live satellite reports or satellite recordings relied on ITN being able to find fixed satellite stations.

In June the rather more conventional ITN Outside Broadcast Unit was sent to cover a dinner at the National Portrait Gallery. It was for the leaders of the G7 countries – the main industrial democracies – who were in London for a summit. During a delay while the officials were trying to arrange a group photo, one of the members of the OB crew, Dennis Crabb, wandered around the gallery before stopping to admire a large painting by an unknown Flemish artist. It showed eleven figures seated round a table. He sensed someone come up to him and stand just behind him. Assuming it was one of his colleagues from the OB truck, Dennis started to say how much he liked the painting. The person behind him answered in a gentle American voice, 'I agree with you, but what exactly is the picture about?' Dennis turned round. It was President Reagan. Then another voice spoke – that of an

ITN cameraman Alan Downes showing a young Prince William how an ENG camera works.

Pamela Armstrong

Pamela Armstrong made her *News at Ten* debut in 1983. Her first full-time job in the media came in 1975 when, as a clerk-typist with Capital Radio, she typed the 'patter' scripts for disc jockeys. Her initiation into broadcasting came a few months later when she was given a regular one-minute spot to talk about the best food buys on Michael Aspel's early morning programme.

By 1977 she was presenting Capital's *London Today*. In 1982 she moved to television as a presenter of Channel 4's health series *Well Being*.

Pamela left ITN in 1986. She has since written several books including a celebration of late motherhood entitled *Beating the Biological Clock*.

**Martyn Lewis at work in an edit suite with picture editor
Mike North.**

English woman. It was the Prime Minister, Margaret Thatcher. She knew the answer to the President's question. 'It shows a very early summit conference, you know – the Somerset House conference of 1604. The men in the picture are Flemish and Spanish delegates who came here to discuss ways to find a more peaceful approach to dealing with one another.' 'Very interesting,' said President Reagan and then he gave Dennis a nudge. 'We think we have problems with you guys – trying to sort out our photo-calls. Just imagine how long these guys had to wait around in those days to get a group picture!'

Prince Edward, on a visit to ITN, meeting Alastair Burnet,
ITN Editor David Nicholas, Sandy Gall, and programme
editor Jill Chisholm.

A huge gas leak from a chemical factory at a Bhopal in
India in December killed 2,000 people. 200,000 others had
to be treated for the effects of the gas.

And Finally...

Lancashire: Graham Wilkie found an unusual way to
train for the rigours of competing in the World Skiing
Championships. To test the wind resistance of his
equipment he strapped himself to the roof rack of a
Jaguar car and was driven along Southport beach.

1985

VIEWERS OF *NEWS AT TEN* on one night in April heard something they shouldn't, in a report by Brent Sadler during that night's lead story about the expulsions of Russian diplomats. Brent was seen – and, rather more importantly, heard – swearing after tripping over the names of the diplomats. Hundreds of people phoned up to complain. So how come the normally unflappable Brent made such a howler? The answer lies not entirely with Mr Sadler – but in the edit room where his report that night was put together. It was a late-breaking story and Brent had rushed down to the Foreign Office to do what is known at ITN as a 'piece to camera' – the section of an item where the reporter appears in vision, standing outside somewhere relevant to the story. Reporters occasionally do take more than one go to deliver their lines correctly and that is what happened that night. Unfortunately, in the rush to assemble Brent's report for the start of the programme no one noticed that his first attempt contained the stumble and the swear word. (See the box on page 99 for more about viewers' calls.)

Brent wasn't the only one getting his tongue in a twist. Pamela Armstrong made viewers giggle reading a boxing item. She said the South African Gerry Coetzee had arrived in Britain for his 'fright' with Frank Bruno.

News at Ten's Alastair Burnet secured the first ever interview with the Prince and Princess of Wales as a

A new form of personal travel, the Sinclair C5, took to the road. Inventor Clive Sinclair's attempt to change the way we get around never really caught on.

married couple but it was a long time coming. By this point they had been married for more than four years. The interview was made into a special ITN programme which was screened in Britain and around the world. One estimate suggested 750 million people had watched it. ITN's cameras were allowed to film them with their young sons in Kensington Palace. The Prince and Princess talked to Alastair about their public duties but more interestingly perhaps about their marriage. The royal couple did, laughingly, admit that they had occasional minor arguments – just like most husbands and wives, as the Prince pointed out. There was little sign that day of the unhappiness that was developing in their marriage.

A few months later, *News at Ten* got another scoop interview, this time with Sara Keays – the secretary who had a twelve-year affair, and then a baby daughter, with the former Conservative Party Chairman Cecil Parkinson. She told viewers that night, 'I hope people will see that I'm a different sort of person from the one they expected. If I did wrong, what about him? He was the one who was married.'

In August *News at Ten* got another slight revamp with a new title sequence which created two minor hiccups. Problem one: the new titles began with a computerized animation of the earth surrounded by a kind of mist. You couldn't see which continent was which, let alone which country was which. You could

The end of a year-long strike. The president of the miners' union, Arthur Scargill, leading his men back to work.

Viewers' calls

News at Ten provokes a lot of response from its viewers – favourable and not so. Every phone call is carefully logged; every letter is carefully read. The range of subjects covered is immense: from accusations of political bias (often from both sides of the fence on the same story) to rather personal requests to newscasters or reporters – those familiar faces in the living room. Sometimes *News at Ten* is criticized for the views of interviewees it has carried, rather than something a reporter or newscaster has said.

A recurring complaint is whether the programme should or shouldn't give football or other sports results just before they are shown on ITV. Whenever the results were given, one section of football fans complained. Whenever they weren't, another section complained that they didn't want to have to stay up waiting to find out the result.

The most serious calls or letters are discussed by senior editors and those requesting information are given replies. There are often ideas for stories which are followed up. (Sometimes that late-night nature of the calls makes their contents unrepeatable!) There are one or two regulars, who call two or three times a week, imparting their views on the news of the day.

All in all, this reversal of the usual flow of information is a vital link with the people *News at Ten* is made for: the viewers.

however see the land masses around the two poles. An eagle-eyed don at Oxford, using the freeze-frame button on his new home video recorder, noticed the poles were upside down. By the time he pointed it out it couldn't be changed.

**Martyn Lewis meeting the Duchess of Kent during his
report on the Helen House hospice for sick children.**

After the image of the earth, the camera appeared to go through the mist to show Europe the right way up – as the ITN logo came up on the screen. Then using real pictures shot by a helicopter the titles showed an aerial zoom over Tower Bridge through a city 'skyscape' to Big Ben. In those days, using a helicopter was pretty new for television and it had been hired at some expense. However, one bit of the helicopter's film wasn't used. That is where problem number two begins. At one stage the title sequence was going to pan across from Big Ben to ITN House. Memos were issued in advance of the helicopter's swoop over ITN, asking staff to switch off all the lights in the building and then – at the appropriate cue – switch them back on again. The effect would be that ITN would suddenly light up.

On the night in question, everything was going according to plan. As the helicopter began its approach, everyone switched off the lights ... well, not quite everyone. As the helicopter got nearer, the building was all in darkness – apart from one office. Through his viewfinder, the cameraman could see two men sitting in a blaze of light in the office of the editor David Nicholas, convivially discussing something – quite probably that night's *News at Ten*. One was David himself. The other was Alastair. The recording was abandoned.

The *News at Ten* production team took delivery of its first ever newsroom computer system, which revolutionized the way the programme was prepared. Up to that point, scripts and running orders had been prepared in more or less the same way since ITN began: that is to say, on typewriters. Journalists writing scripts for transmission would

The Tottenham riots and their aftermath. They broke out after the death of a black woman during a police search of her flat. Hundreds went on the rampage. P.C. Keith Blakelock was hacked to death by the mob.

type them out on special paper that would make three copies – it worked in the same way as carbon paper. The programme's chief sub editor would then make his or her amendments to that script with a biro, and then hand it to the newscasters. They too would make the changes they wanted before the sheets were handed to typists. They would type out a nice, new, clear version on grey paper – a colour chosen because it didn't reflect the studio lights. The new Basys computer system changed all that. Now the journalists could write the script into a computer.

It could be looked at and changed by the chief sub and then by the newscaster without a piece of paper ever being needed. When the newscaster had finished looking at the script, he or she pressed a button on their keyboard and the script printed out automatically on a printer. It meant fewer typists were needed but it speeded up and streamlined the process of producing scripts. Journalists were able to work faster and push deadlines ever closer towards transmission time.

The new system also gave every journalist in the building instant access to news agency reports from around the world. And since then, newsroom computers have moved on even further. ITN is now taking delivery of computers that can edit pictures as well as words.

And Finally...

A Cambridge policeman decided the best way to raise money for charity was to jump off the top of the Telecom Tower in London. However, he wasn't alone. A team of Royal Marines joined him in the abseiling event.

    PC Gill Boyd descended 500 feet to get himself into the record books as well as collecting £10,000 for Great Ormond Street Hospital.

1986

I N THE SUMMER Pamela Armstrong announced she was leaving *News at Ten* after nearly three years and went to the BBC, to present a daytime chat show and magazine programme. Within a few weeks Martyn Lewis said he too was going to the BBC – to read their *One O'Clock News*. This time there was to be no big outside search for replacements. Carol Barnes – who had been presenting ITN's early evening news – was to join the *News at Ten* team.

When the Chinese government decided to invite the Queen to make an extensive royal tour of the country, ITN's editor David Nicholas was determined that ITN would take full advantage of the occasion and produce a special half-hour programme every day from the various cities the Queen was visiting. That would be relatively straightforward from places like Beijing and Canton, but what about other smaller and more remote cities? And what about the historic moment when the Queen set foot on the Great Wall of China? That too would make an excellent live programme but it could be done only with a mobile satellite dish.

The negotiations with the Chinese authorities took several months and eventually ITN and the BBC were allowed to send reconnaissance parties to do an advance tour of the Royal route. No trial tests of equipment were allowed so ITN had to rely on a set of calculations by station engineer Peter Heaps. He seemed to be using only a basic compass and a few mathematical calculations. On these simple sums, ITN was to commit several hundred thousand

pounds! Those sums proved to be right. For the first time, the world saw live pictures from the Great Wall of China.

The satellite dish had to be slung below a Chinese army helicopter and flown to the wall from Beijing. What the calculations hadn't included was the possibility of fog. The weather closed in and it proved impossible to move the dish from the wall to the next stop of the Queen's visit, Kunming. It wasn't just the ITN team that was worried about what would happen if the fog didn't lift. The dish was also being used by both the BBC and *TV-am* for live and recorded reports. Luckily for everyone, the weather changed and the dish managed to reach Kunming with less than an hour to spare.

The satellite dish proved its effectiveness again the following November, but in far from celebratory circumstances. *News at Ten* covered a terrible helicopter crash – a Chinook was carrying Shell workers from the Brent oil field back to Sumburgh airport on the Shetland Islands when it came down two miles off the coast. ITN chartered a Lear jet and flew reporter Simon Cole and his crew to Shetland. Covering any breaking story from there is difficult because there is no satellite station on the islands. So ITN hired a Shackleton cargo plane and flew the satellite dish to the island. It was set up just south of Sumburgh airport. This meant it was possible to create up-to-the-minute reports. It cut out the need to fly reports from Shetland to Aberdeen, as other news

organizations had to. ITN's coverage of the crash easily outstripped the opposition's.

By the summer, the newsroom computer system had been up and running for a year. There had been one or two teething problems but the computers had been a great aid to the production process. It did completely break down in April, though, the day the Duchess of Windsor – Wallis Simpson – died. Journalists had to run round the building to find typewriters so they could write and prepare the story. The newsroom had been a much quieter place since the computers arrived. Suddenly there was the familiar sound of old technology filling the place.

Sometimes humans can cause a breakdown in communications all by themselves. When the

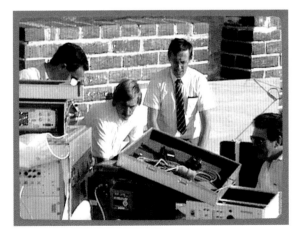

The ITN satellite dish was guided down onto the Great Wall of China from a helicopter by engineer Fred Rich. Once set up the ITN team had to check it was broadcasting pictures back to London.

Martyn Lewis, CBE

Born in Wales and brought up in Northern Ireland, Martyn Lewis began his television career with the BBC in Belfast in 1967 after graduating from Trinity College, Dublin. He joined HTV in Cardiff as a reporter a year later, moving to ITN in 1970. He set up its Northern Bureau, and returned to London in 1978 to combine the roles of foreign correspondent and newscaster. He became a regular co-presenter of *News at Ten* in 1982.

During his time at *News at Ten* Martyn Lewis was involved in the coverage of two royal weddings, the Pope's visit to Britain, and the Falklands War. He also made many foreign reporting assignments for ITN.

In 1986, after sixteen years with ITN he left to present BBC1's *One O'Clock News*. Two years later he became a presenter of the *Nine O'Clock News* on BBC1. In 1994 he moved to the *Six O'Clock News*. He is also the presenter of *Today's the Day* on BBC2. He made headlines in 1993 with his much-criticized campaign for more good news stories.

He is the author of many books and is involved with several charitable organizations. In 1997 he was awarded the CBE for services to young people and the hospice movement.

Martyn Lewis and Pamela Armstrong in the *News at Ten* studio.

American clarinettist Benny Goodman died in June viewers were almost told someone else had passed away. When first reports appeared on the teleprinters, that night's copytaster, the person who looks through all the reports to see which stories might make it on to *News at Ten*, told his colleagues, 'The king of swing is dead.' A script writer misheard him and thought he'd said, 'The King of Sweden is dead.' A slide of the King of Sweden was requested.

The confusion didn't end there. The stills librarian called back, 'He's with his coronet. Is that OK?' That was misheard too. The scriptwriter thought the librarian had said 'clarinet' and replied 'OK'. So what the viewers nearly heard was a story about the death of the King of Sweden with a picture of His Majesty holding his coronet. Fortunately, someone spotted the mix-up and a diplomatic incident with Stockholm was averted.

And Finally...

The players of the England versus Holland hockey game knew they were destined to play on a damp pitch and would definitely end the game soaked. However, this had nothing whatsoever to do with English weather.

The match, to be held in the swimming pool of the St Albans Mears Club, was an international contest in the underwater hockey championships.

1987

ALASTAIR BURNET'S presentation of *News at Ten* could never be faulted – apart perhaps from one night in March when he started losing his voice during the programme because of a cold. He started off well enough – alongside Carol Barnes – reading the top story about the Queen's banquet for King Fahd. He said later his voice had been all right during the day but started to go just as he was about to go on air. 'All of a sudden, it cracked,' he said. 'I managed to struggle through mainly because Carol did most of the hard work.' He even had to let her read the football results. Carol said, 'Alastair handed me the scripts and I had to read the second half virtually by myself.' Alastair did of course manage to round off the programme with a croaky 'Goodnight'.

By now, ITN headquarters in Wells Street was getting a little cramped to cope with the expanding empire. The company decided it was time for another move. ITN's next home was to be on the site of the *Sunday Times* building in Gray's Inn Road, in Central London. First though the *Sunday Times* building would be pulled down and a new one – designed by the architect Sir Norman Foster – would be erected in its place. The design work, construction and equipping was to take three years.

There was some rather more rudimentary construction and equipping already going on in ITN's new Moscow bureau. Until now, events in Moscow had been covered by reporters from London – working out of hotel rooms – assuming of course they were allowed in. The rapidly changing story and the new Gorbachev era of *glasnost* dictated a more permanent arrangement. Apart from filing reports, the new ITN team had to fit-out the bureau.

First of all they had to knock down the walls of the apartment they'd chosen to make a bit more room to work in. Their first desk was a fifty-gallon oil drum. They placed the telex on top of the drum and left the phone on the floor. Communication by phone – particularly with London – was a hit-and-miss affair. On top of that, there weren't any Moscow phone books so they couldn't ring many people anyway. The telex was a more reliable way of contacting people – even people in different parts of Moscow.

They also kept a set of spare tyres in the bureau because often theirs got stolen. They bought generators from Finland to power the edit gear. The only place for the generator to go was on the balcony – which was against fire regulations. They also bought workbenches and shelves and assembled them all. Reporter Ian Glover-James put up shelves while editor Roger Pittman rewired the apartment to take the electrical strain created by the edit gear. Once the bureau was up and working there was still no satellite station nearby. They had to drive from central Moscow to a suburb to file their reports. It wasn't until the following year that a satellite dish was set up in the centre of the city.

Michael Brunson reporting the news from parliament.

In the general election campaign back home *News at Ten* decided to amend slightly the target team approach that had worked so well in the 1983 general election. Each party leader would still have one reporter assigned to him or her but political editor Michael Brunson was to be freed up from editing reports all day so he could get out and find out what was happening. When he was told he was going to do live reports every night instead of recorded ones Michael said he wasn't very keen on the idea. He didn't think he'd do them very well. On this rare occasion Michael was wrong. In fact he did do them very well and 'live two-ways' as they are known are one of his fortes.

Mrs Thatcher won her third general election in a row – the first prime minister to do so for over a century. It had been a frantic campaign as party leaders criss-crossed the country. The team covering the campaign of Labour leader Neil Kinnock found themselves thwarted by the elements as they tried to send one report back from Anglesey. Jon Snow had edited his report – which was to be the main story on that night's *News at Ten* – and they were driving to the satellite truck to send it back to London. The truck was on top of a hill and clearly visible – until the fog came down. Finding it suddenly became a big problem. The team drove around at break-neck speed. Finally, they found it with five minutes to spare and handed the tape to the engineer to send to London. Only when he tried to do so did he discover that the fog had got into the equipment as well and the tape wouldn't play. So no lead story. And life and limb had been risked for nothing.

In the middle of the year Julia Somerville joined ITN – though not at that stage the *News at Ten* team – from the BBC. She had been reading their *Nine O'Clock News* and was now to present ITN's *News at 12.30*.

Nearly two hundred people died when the cross-channel ferry, the *Herald of Free Enterprise*, sank off Zeebrugge. It had set off from the port with its bow doors open, allowing water to flood the car deck.

Royal visits have always been part of *News at Ten*'s life. When Princess Margaret came round to watch the programme going out there was, as usual after a VIP visit, a little refreshment in the studio afterwards. The Princess chatted to the presenters and to the senior editors who were on duty that night. During the conversation she had lit a cigarette and as she smoked it, not surprisingly, the ash on the end of the cigarette got longer and longer. She seemed to look round for an ashtray. Suddenly one of the scene shifters, Bert Jellicoe, appeared at her side with an ash-tray. The Princess thanked him and Bert – a dapper man in his sixties – smiled at the Princess and tried to engage her in conversation. He said how pleased he was to see her and how he wished he had known, before he set off for work, that she was going to be visiting ITN that night. The Princess asked him why. 'Well,' replied Bert, 'I met you in 1942 during the war along with your sister and your late father the King.' 'Oh really,' the Princess replied and lit another cigarette. 'Yes,' continued Bert, 'if I'd known, I could have brought in some photographs of our previous meeting.' The Princess smiled at Bert and he, needing no more encouragement, began telling her some of his many war stories. Bert began to drift

slightly away from the main group and to the surprise of those around, the Princess followed him. Their conversation lasted another ten minutes or so. No one knows whether she was genuinely interested in his war time recollections or whether she just wanted to remain close to an ashtray.

And Finally...

Proficiency at any sport is a mixture of skills, natural talent and the dedication to train, train, train. The Australian bob-sled team, preparing for the 1998 Winter Olympics, were no exception. They had the drive and the will to win – they just didn't have any snow to practise on!

Undeterred, they came up with a simple solution. They built a sled on wheels and practised their starts in the car park of Woolworth's in Sydney.

Carol Barnes

Carol Barnes was born in 1944 and brought up in Tooting, South London.

She studied French and Spanish at Sheffield University and after graduating she became managing editor of *Time Out*, and was a founder member of the London Broadcasting Company.

Carol joined ITN as a reporter in 1975 from BBC Radio 4's *World at One*. Her reporting work has been very varied – she covered the troubles in Belfast; and in 1982, when seven months pregnant, she found herself reporting on the Brixton riots. She was assigned to follow Geraldine Ferraro's campaign during the US presidential election of 1984, and was part of the ITN team covering the Royal Weddings in 1981 and 1986.

Carol, who is known to her colleagues as Barnsie, began newscasting in 1979. She was one of the main newscasters on *News at Ten* from September 1986 until she became the presenter of ITN's *Channel 4 Daily* in 1989. She then moved to ITN's *News at 5.40* and later bacame one of the presenters of ITN's weekend bulletins on ITV and the occasional *Lunchtime News*.

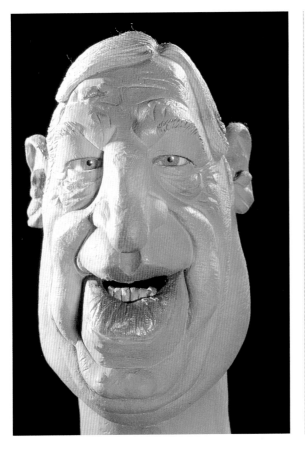

The *News at Ten* presenters became a regular part of the *Spitting Image* programme during the 1980s: Alastair Burnet interviewing the Labour leader Neil Kinnock (top left), Trevor McDonald's puppet (bottom left), Sandy Gall (above left), Martyn Lewis (above right) and Alastair Burnet (below).

1988

THE TELEVISION HISTORY of Northern Ireland's thirty years of troubles is a bloody one. One shocking incident among too many was played out in front of ITN cameras in March. Two British soldiers – both army corporals from the Signals regiment – had inadvertently driven their car into the path of an IRA funeral procession. By the time they had realized what they had done, so had some of the crowd around them. The next few chilling moments were filmed by ITN. A mob pulled the two men from their Volkswagen Passat and began to attack them. They were beaten, stripped then shot. Their bodies were dumped on waste ground.

Usually television news cameras record the aftermath of events like these. The power of the pictures that day was immense. It led to a huge public and political clamour for the killers to be found. Once again ITN found itself under pressure from the police – the Royal Ulster Constabulary on this occasion – to hand over all the film that was shot, not just what appeared in the night's programme. Once again ITN resisted – insisting if it gave unseen footage to the police it was risking the safety of its crews, because they could be viewed as working for the police. Once again, it ended with legal moves to force ITN to hand over its pictures.

More new technology was on its way – one-man cameras. In the past, crews had consisted of a cameraman, sound engineer and, sometimes, a lighting engineer. The new cameras wouldn't replace all two- or three-man crews but it would replace some of them. It would mean job losses and some savings for the company but there were certainly journalistic advantages.

Take for example the old U-matic camera in the Moscow bureau. When the temperature dropped drastically – as in the long Russian winter – its batteries could produce only half the power. Also, in the many demonstrations that were going on in Moscow at the time, Soviet security men would often try and stop crews filming by snatching the cable that connected the camera to the recorder held by the sound engineer. In the new Beta cameras, the video cassette which recorded the pictures and the sound was inside the camera – just like on a home camcorder. The Moscow bureau had a crew of two. When two new cameras arrived it meant they could both film stories – so one camera could stay in Moscow in case anything happened to President Gorbachev, while the other could go off filming.

Back in the *News at Ten* studio there were changes to the cameras too. Some studio cameramen were to be replaced, by robotic cameras that could be controlled from a panel in the control room. Studio camera operators would still be needed but not as many.

Taken together, the changes brought about by new technology meant over 140 staff were to lose their jobs. These were changing times at ITN, which had always belonged to the ITV regional companies. Now

Shots rang out during an IRA funeral at Milltown cemetery in Belfast. A loyalist gunman opened fire on mourners, killing three people and wounding fifty others.

there was talk that ITN should be sold off and have outside shareholders as well.

December saw two big disaster stories within nine days. First came the Clapham rail disaster in south-west London. Thirty-five people were killed when a faulty signal led to a packed commuter service crashing into the back of another train – and then a third empty train ran into the wreckage. It was a tragic story to report but had none of the logistic problems of the second tragedy that month. That came on the evening of 21 December. A Pan-Am Jumbo jet – Flight 103 – had left Heathrow for New York at 6.25pm – twenty-five minutes later than

scheduled. It had reached its cruising altitude of 31,000 feet as it was crossing the Scottish Borders, close to a then little-known town called Lockerbie, ready to head out across the Atlantic. At 7.19pm it disappeared from radar screens. Back at ITN, the news desk began getting reports of what was then thought to be a light plane crash. When the newsdesk checked out the reports they were told initially that two RAF planes had crashed into one another. Obviously that would have been a news story but nothing on the scale of the disaster that then unfolded. It soon became clear the plane had been blown up by a terrorist bomb. If it had gone off a few minutes later, the plane would have been out over the sea. Those on the plane would still have died but Lockerbie would have remained the quiet Borders town it was earlier that day.

The disaster happened on the night of the ITN managers' Christmas party in an Italian restaurant near ITN House. They and their partners were wearing party hats and enjoying themselves when suddenly everyone's bleepers went off at the same time. Within seconds only the partners were left at the tables as the news editors headed back to work. The owner of the restaurant was worried they didn't like his food.

The Clapham rail disaster in south-west London killed thirty-five people.

The cockpit of Pan Am Jumbo jet *Maid of the Seas* lying on a hillside outside Lockerbie.

News at Ten's nearest reporter that night was Mark Webster – then north of England correspondent based in Manchester. When it became clear what had happened, he was sent to the scene. Needless to say, when he got there it took him ages to get close, because so many emergency vehicles were there. He made it to the scene with moments to spare to give a phoned report during *News at Ten*. In those days mobile phones weren't quite so common. Mark used the mobile phone in the crew car. By this point the car couldn't get any nearer the scene anyway. All four tyres had burst from driving over the debris.

Mark remembers the smoke being extraordinarily thick. So much so that when he went to the town's pub to book a room he was so covered in soot that the staff there thought he had been involved in some way in the accident.

Mark wasn't quite so effective on another assignment that year – a report on pioneering eye surgery at a hospital in Birmingham. A Russian specialist had come to Selly Oak Hospital to perform the five-minute operation which corrected short-sightedness. Mark takes up the story. 'The professor was describing in detail how you make an incision into the eye and I was watching the operation on a huge screen at the same time. The two things together were too much and something inside me just clicked and I fainted. I hit my head on a door stopper and needed nine stitches. It was all very embarrassing. I had to be wheeled out of the operating theatre. I'd covered operations before but nothing like this had ever happened.'

News at Ten's normal appetite for sports news was sharpened by scandal during the big sporting story of the year, the Seoul Olympics. The Canadian sprinter, Ben Johnson, became the fastest man on earth with a new world record time for the 100 metres of 9.79 seconds. That seemed a big enough story in itself. But soon afterwards that medal was to be taken from Johnson when he tested positive for drugs.

The night before news of the drugs test came through, the ITN team in Seoul had been having dinner in the Hilton hotel. They had filed their reports for that night's *News at Ten* because Seoul was ten hours ahead of London time. Sitting at the next table in the Hilton restaurant was Ben Johnson and a coterie of agents, advisers and lawyer, perhaps deciding how to cash in on Johnson's amazing feat – and amazing feet. One of the ITN crew, Jim Dutton, went over to Johnson's table to get him to sign his menu. Little did the ITN team know what would happen next. They enjoyed the rest of their evening, retiring to their rooms at around half-past three in the morning Seoul time.

An hour later the news editor in Seoul, Nigel Hancock, got the news about the drugs test. He phoned reporters Mark Austin and Peter Staunton to tell them. They thought it was a joke. Even when a call came through from *News at Ten* in London, they thought it was all part of an elaborate prank. When it finally sank in they rapidly had to file new reports to make the deadline for *News at Ten*. The programme's coverage that night involved Alastair Burnet in the *News at Ten* studio doing a live

Alastair Burnet presenting a special programme on Australia's bicentennial celebrations (above). The Prince and Princess of Wales and hundreds of tall ships were there to mark the occasion. Alastair off duty down under (right).

interview with Mark Austin who had had one hour's sleep and hadn't had time to shave. Alastair ended his introduction to Mark with the words '… it is early in the morning in Seoul, as you can see.'

One other item of sports news – golf. In the Open at Lytham, an ITN camera buggy found itself in Nick Faldo's firing line on the seventeenth hole in more ways than one. One ITN camera buggy was right behind Faldo who was trying to hit out of a bunker. He was psyched-up and didn't like the slightest noise distracting him. Everyone held their breath as he prepared to swing at the ball. Suddenly he stopped as a second ITN buggy went lurching across the fairway. Its crew didn't know the first buggy was already with Faldo and was trying to get to him. The golfer started

to shout, 'What is that over there?' The crew next to him said nothing but tried to radio buggy number two to get it to stop. When it did stop, Faldo played a terrible shot out of the bunker. He didn't find out until some time later whose buggy it was.

Carol Barnes's fear of flying had occasionally taken the fun out of foreign assignments on trips to Europe and the United States. So she decided to try to overcome her fear by learning to fly herself. She started taking lessons at Shoreham airport near her home in Brighton in a Cessna 152, and then took some more during a holiday in Florida. It took her forty hours' flying time to get her pilot's licence, but the most nerve-racking moment was on the day she was doing her final cross-country flight – the flight that would decide whether or not she got her licence. She was heading for Southend airport when she got completely lost in low cloud. She didn't know which way she was going. A controller at Southend airport tried to talk her down but, just to make things even worse, her radio was cutting out as well. In the end she landed safely and won special praise for her level-headedness in a difficult situation. Suffice to say, she passed her test with 'flying colours'.

If you were looking for the perfect Christmas present for the news junkie among your family or friends, *News at Ten* had the answer. It was a *News at Ten* board game. Players had to pretend to dash around the world collecting stories, pictures and headlines to make up the items for a news programme.

Also out that Christmas the *News at Ten* acid house dance single, though that was *not* made by ITN. After a report on the programme about the new drugs and dance craze, a record company pirated the voices of Alastair, Sandy and reporter Penny Marshall to form part of the lyrics.

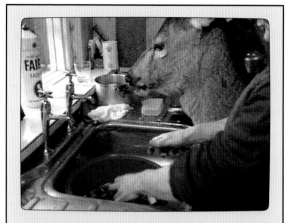

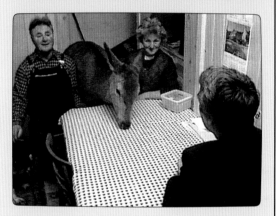

And Finally...

A farmer and his wife at Dallas, Morayshire, Scotland, were very proud of their eighteen-month-old baby, Barbie. Already a precocious youngster, Barbie liked to help around the kitchen, particularly eating the potato peelings.

The young red deer also had a taste for oven-fresh scones, which meant it was already getting close to its optimum weight of twenty stone.

Barbie, who did not seem to believe he was a deer, would go out with the farmer's wife when she walked and would ride behind the tractor when they took feed to the other animals on the farm.

1989

L IKE A HOUSE OF CARDS, it seemed, communist governments across Eastern Europe were collapsing. They were momentous days for the people of those countries and for the people who reported on them. The fall of the Berlin Wall happened in front of our eyes and our cameras. *News at Ten* had been covering the story of the demise of East Germany's leader Eric Honecker. He hadn't seen the metaphorical writing on the wall when the people of the Eastern bloc started pressing for more freedom and greater contact with the West. Even when the Soviet President Mikhail Gorbachev told Mr Honecker he had to move with the times, he refused to bend. In the end he was ousted by his own Communist Party.

When the announcement came that the gates and checkpoints along the Wall were to be opened in November, the people of East Berlin couldn't believe it. The ITN crew there heard a kind of low rumbling sound as, literally, the news spread from person to person. The rumble became a roar and within seconds people were out on the streets cheering and shouting for joy.

Once the news had sunk in, many of the East Berliners quickly decided what they most wanted to do now they could leave their sector of the city: they wanted to get their first taste of life in the West by going to the big shopping centre in West Berlin. The East German soldiers on the Brandenburg Gate were

News at Ten reported the historic fall of the Berlin Wall in December 1989.

also taken aback by the order to open the gate and didn't quite know what to do.

ITN decided to send in some of its top reporters and presenters. Jon Snow, John Suchet and Alastair Stewart were flown in on a special charter plane from Gatwick. When they all appeared together standing on top of a platform in front of the Brandenburg Gate on the monitors in the newsroom, someone said, 'There they are. The "Egos" have landed!'

ITN programmes took live reports from all three as they stood in front of the wall. They also compiled their own recorded reports. John Suchet's assignment for one was to find a family crossing for the first time from East to West. He was in West

Jon Snow, Alastair Stewart and John Suchet covered the
fall of the Berlin Wall from in front of the Brandenburg
Gate (above). John Suchet reporting in front of the
Berlin Wall (right).

Berlin and had been told there were no guards on
the eastern side of the wall so there'd be no
problem getting across to find a suitable family.
As he and his crew drove up to the border there
were guards there. John told them he and the crew
were tourists. The guard was clearly suspicious. He
asked if they had any television cameras. John lied
– in the interests of ITN of course – and said, 'No.'
The guard asked to open the boot. At that moment,
John was mentally preparing his telex to the foreign
desk. 'Sorry. Mission failed. We are on our way
home.' It didn't come to that, though. The guard
looked inside the boot, saw the camera, then
winked, wished the team good luck and waved
them through.

They found an East German family who were actually from Rostock on East Germany's northern coast. They were on holiday in East Berlin – the height of sophistication compared to Rostock. When John and his team accompanied them through to the western sector they couldn't believe their eyes as they walked along the main shopping street, the Kurfustendamm. What they most wanted to buy was trainers. They had clearly felt rather uncomfortable and out of place as they struggled to adjust to the ways of the West. As the day drew to an end, one of the family complained of a headache and wanted some painkillers. They went to the chemist's in the underground station but there was a long queue. John said he knew another chemist's nearby where they wouldn't have to queue. 'No,' they said, they were quite happy queuing. It was what they were used to. For the first time all day they looked genuinely happy.

ITN's camera crews in an unprecedented get-together for a group photograph.

Within days of the Berlin Wall being opened, there were big changes too in Czechoslovakia. First came huge protest marches and rallies. The violence was small-scale. It became known as the Velvet Revolution. The Communist government resigned en masse when they saw the way things were going. Crowds thronged the centre of the capital, Prague, and packed into Wenceslas Square to welcome back Alexander Dubcek – the Czechoslovak leader who twenty years earlier had tried and failed to resist Russian domination in what became known as the Prague Spring.

An anti-Communist playwright called Vaclav Havel, recently released from jail, was to become the country's new president. It was a big story. Alastair Stewart was sent to Prague to do live reports. The only place he could do them was from an American camera position. There was, however, a problem. The Americans didn't have an actual camera. So Alastair had to borrow an American home video camera. The

Alastair Stewart

Alastair studied economics, politics and sociology at Bristol University and was deputy president of the National Union of Students from 1974 to 1976.

He began his career in broadcasting with Southern Television in 1976, where he was a reporter, industrial correspondent, presenter and documentary maker.

Alastair joined ITN as an industrial correspondent in 1980. He spent three years as a presenter and reporter for ITN's *Channel 4 News* and *The Parliament Programme*. He presented the *News at 5.40* and then joined *News at Ten* in May 1989. After a year as ITN's Washington correspondent he resumed his role as *News at Ten* newscaster in 1991 until its relaunch with a single anchor in 1992.

During the Gulf War he reported and anchored *News at Ten* from Dhahran and the newly liberated Kuwait City.

Alastair left ITN in 1992 for London News Network where he presents *London Tonight*. He is also the presenter of ITV's *Police Camera Action* and GMTV's *The Sunday Programme*.

pictures had to be sent to New York via a tiny satellite dish and then back across the Atlantic to London. No one at ITN ever noticed they weren't the normal high quality television signals.

When the story finished the ITN crews returned to London. Most had Christmas on their minds. But big news stories don't respect holiday times as the next revolution, in Romania, proved only too well. ITN sent two teams to Romania – one with reporter Paul Davies, the other with his colleague Colin Baker.

Paul had only just returned from Czechoslovakia when he was asked to go to the Romanian capital Bucharest. No commercial planes were flying in because of the fighting that had broken out between the Communist forces loyal to dictator Nicolae Ceausescu and the anti-government rebels. ITN chartered a small plane to fly Paul and his crew to Bucharest airport. As they entered Romanian airspace, the control tower told them they couldn't land there because of the fighting. As Paul remembers, 'Our pilot then produced a brilliant performance, persuading controllers that our fuel was critically low because we'd only ever planned to get as far as Bucharest. We were allowed to land.'

The next problem was how to get into the city. Some supporters of the revolution took them by bus to the outskirts of the city and they made a base camp at a hotel there. The people in the hotel warned Paul and his team that it was dangerous to go into the city, but

Paul wanted to check whether the television station there was still working and the crew agreed to come with him. When they got there the building was surrounded by hundreds of students and other young anti-Ceausescu protesters. While Paul and his crew were inside the television station it came under attack from Ceausescu forces. 'We were pinned down there for the whole of that night,' says Paul, 'but we were in the fortunate position of being the only people in Romania able to broadcast news of the battle happening around us.'

The fight for the television station continued for three or four days. The ITN team slipped out of the building after the first night, taking their pictures back to the hotel. Unfortunately it proved much more difficult to get back into the building for a second night. However, they were helped by a group of young Romanians who knew that the videocassette in Paul's hand was the only record of the sacrifice made by many of their friends the night before. 'That helped us get back in, through what was now a fierce battle for the television station,' says Paul. To get there, they had to drive through a square, across which the two sides were firing at each other. They stuck a white flag out of the window and crouched in the bottom of the car. They then couldn't get from the car to the television station because of the gunfire. They spent their second night lying underneath an armoured car just outside the television station listening to the gunfire and the occasional bullets bouncing off the vehicle they were sheltering under. 'Once we got inside,' said Paul, 'we made the group decision that more journeys like that would not be a good idea!'

They set up camp inside one of the studios, where they remained for the best part of two weeks. As Paul says, 'We were better able to report what was happening in Romania than anyone else because we were at the centre of one of the fiercest power struggles.' There was another advantage to being inside the television station. It was being used as a

Paul Davies reporting on the upheavals in Romania.

headquarters for the people who were trying to topple Ceausescu. They held their meetings in rooms alongside the studios. They gave Paul briefings on the latest developments. The ITN team even saw two of Ceausescu's children being dragged in to be questioned. 'It was just the place to be,' says Paul. Underlying all that was the fact that Paul could broadcast more or less when he or ITN wanted, with the help of the friends they were now making among the staff of Romanian television. He used the same set as the leaders of the revolution were using to tell the people outside what was going on. In the background was a Romanian flag which had had its central motif of a Soviet hammer and sickle symbolically torn out.

In all this time Christmas was getting nearer and that added to the emotion of the story. 'We woke up on Christmas morning, from another night of lying on our makeshift beds on the studio floor, to discover that the Romanian television people had managed to smuggle in a few loaves of bread and some local cheese. That was to be our Christmas breakfast, lunch and dinner. Someone also produced a hip flask,' says Paul. 'I do remember on Christmas Day having to crawl along an exposed glass walkway to get to the toilet. Also, I particularly remember seeing a man who worked at the

Paul Davies, pictured left, in the Bucharest television studio with Romanian presenter Victor Ionescu.

television station and who we'd befriended. He'd just been told that his house had been hit on the night of Christmas Eve and that two of his children had been killed. That was our Christmas.'

Not surprisingly, after sharing so much, Paul became very close friends with the staff of

Romanian television, in particular El-Marie Ionescu – who ran the international department – and her husband Victor who was a senior newscaster and political correspondent. El-Marie always made sure Paul's broadcasts got through to London whatever was happening outside the building. Victor was for many Romanian television viewers one of the faces of the revolution. Victor's jacket had got dirty and there was no way of getting a new one. So he and Paul took it in turns to wear Paul's jacket as they did their broadcasts.

When it was all over and Paul was back in London ITN organized a small celebration to mark the success of the coverage. What Paul didn't know was that there were some surprise guests. They were the Ionescus. They had brought with them a souvenir for Paul. It was the Romanian flag – with the hammer

Paul Davies, second from left, and ITN colleague Penny Marshall, right, with the Ionescus at a party in London arranged by ITN. The Ionescus presented Paul with the flag from the Bucharest television station.

and sickle torn out – that had flown from the television station and which became a symbol of those momentous weeks.

The story of Colin Baker and his team is equally dramatic. The revolution actually began with a protest in a town called Timisoara. It was, as both Paul and Colin were to report, to topple the most severe regime in Eastern Europe. Colin and his team, including Sue Tinson who was then *News at Ten*'s programme editor, set off slightly after Paul in a larger plane carrying other journalists and the ITN satellite dish, hoping to reach Timisoara. While they were in the air it became apparent, as Paul had found, that this was to be a more bloody revolution than the recent Velvet Revolution in nearby Czechoslovakia. Fighting on the ground meant they were refused permission to land and had to divert to Budapest in Hungary. An advance party, including reporter Penny Marshall, had

already been into Timisoara but was now back on the Hungarian border.

An ITN team in Budapest had managed to hire a lorry and came to meet Colin's flight and unload all the gear, including of course the satellite dish. Before setting off for Romania they loaded up with the essentials of life: petrol, baked beans and Spam. As they approached the border, they were listening to the radio which was reporting the gunfire on the Romanian side. The driver said he didn't want to cross so ITN agreed to hire the lorry from its owners for $5,000 and said it would be brought back in three days' time. By now the ITN team had assembled something of a convoy of hire cars, a four-wheel drive and the lorry. Using masking tape, they made signs saying 'TV' in the hope of not being shot at. Those in the cars made it across the border and then through the gunfire to Timisoara and arrived at the town's only hotel which was completely deserted and pretty low on food. The lorry took rather longer, but it was cheered – or so the team on board thought – by

Christmas lunch for the *News at Ten* team in Timisoara, Romania – Spam, baked beans and something to drink.

Cameraman Sebastian Rich and reporter Desmond Hamill in Sudan. Floods there left thousands of people homeless and without food or clean water.

Romanian wellwishers who had seen the 'TV' signs. In fact the people were warning them to turn back as the lorry was heading into 'snipers' alley'. When the lorry finally arrived at the hotel it was covered in bullet marks, but fortunately no one was hurt.

Once everyone had calmed down, they asked if they could put the satellite dish on the roof of the hotel. Whenever it was used it had unfortunate consequences for the townspeople of Timisoara. The dish used all of the electricity that was reaching the town and blacked it out for the duration of the broadcast. Colin Baker did his live reports on the roof in the full glare of ITN's lights, with all the surrounding area in darkness. It was a frightening way to broadcast because it made him something of a target. Eventually they managed to get a generator. Christmas Day in Timisoara was very cold but celebrated with the baked beans and Spam and

a little champagne which the ITN team had been given in exchange for some of their Spam.

Trevor McDonald was despatched to Romania to present *News at Ten* from there. The satellite dish therefore had to move from Timisoara to Bucharest. The live camera position was outside the British Embassy there. Much planning had gone into the operation. Needless to say, seeing and hearing Trevor was vital if the programme was going to work. But although Trevor was in position in Bucharest the *News at Ten* control room could neither see nor hear him. With twenty seconds to go Julia Somerville – in the studio in London – was preparing to read the introductions to the items that Trevor was meant to read. Then suddenly, thanks to some frantic checking of snowbound cables in Bucharest, Trevor appeared. What's more, he could hear studio talkback and delivered his lines as though there had never been a problem.

To get everyone back when the story was over ITN hired one large charter plane with over a hundred

Moscow Correspondent Ian Glover-James and his family at Heathrow having been expelled by the Soviet Union.

seats – the idea being that ITN could help fly out other journalists too to defray the cost. There then followed a string of phone calls to foreign editor Mike Nolan in Bucharest, during which he was repeatedly heard to ask 'Aisle or window seat? Smoking or non-smoking?'

Ian Glover-James, *News at Ten*'s Moscow Correspondent, found himself caught up in a diplomatic row between Britain and the Soviet Union in May. The British government had ordered the expulsion of eleven diplomats and journalists for spying. The Kremlin hit back, ordering out eleven Britons – eight diplomats and three journalists. Ian was one of the journalists. It was the last diplomatic expulsion row between Britain and the Soviet Union of the Cold War. Apart from the fact that neither Ian nor any other journalists had, as the Kremlin claimed, been spying, it was especially hard for correspondents to be asked to leave when history was being made in the Soviet Union by President Gorbachev's reforms. Ian was at his flat in Moscow when the phone rang one Sunday morning. It was the First Secretary at the British Embassy on the phone. It was obviously going to be a call of some importance for it to be made at that time on a

Sandy Gall filming in Afghanistan with Mujahideen fighters opposed to the Soviet occupation.

Sunday. The First Secretary asked Ian to come to the embassy. He guessed what might be coming when he saw, in his rear view mirror, *The Sunday Times* correspondent pulling up behind him outside the embassy. They were joined by the BBC correspondent in the large drawing room of the embassy and the First Secretary told them they were being expelled by the Soviet authorities and had fourteen days in which to get out. As Ian says, 'It was a very peculiar situation. There I was reporting on myself, before I had to leave.' There was also the rather curious experience for Ian of seeing himself written about by Tass, the Soviet news agency, which was issuing untrue reports about his spying. Once those reports got into Moscow newspapers and on to Soviet television Ian got some very suspicious looks from his neighbours.

The mandarins of Moscow had other things on their mind. The Soviet Union was pulling its troops out of Afghanistan after nearly ten years of occupation. It was a humiliating climbdown. *News at Ten* sent three reporting teams to cover the withdrawal. Sandy Gall left his seat in the studio to travel from Pakistan across the border to Afghanistan. Part of his equipment was a satellite dish which could be collapsed into pieces and be transported on the backs of two or three horses. Sandy's remarkable reports gave a real feel of what it was like to be with the Mujahideen trekking through the mountains as the Soviet Union withdrew.

Sandy's live reports became a regular feature of ITN programmes and of American television too. On one occasion, he was asked to 'go live' for an American breakfast television programme. Sandy could hear the presenter in New York reporting the withdrawal and then handing over like this: 'With us this morning we have ITN's correspondent in Jalalabad Sandy Gall and she joins us now from Afghanistan live. Good morning, Sandy.' Sandy was too much of a gentleman to draw attention to the mistake in New York as, after all, Sandy can be a girl's name.

Carol Barnes ended her stint as a *News at Ten* presenter in April – though she wasn't leaving ITN. She was to be the new presenter of *Channel Four Daily*, a breakfast programme with a mix of business, arts, entertainment and consumer stories as well as news headlines. In her place, from ITN's *Lunchtime News* came Julia Somerville. She achieved the rare distinction of becoming the first women to present the country's two main evening news programme: *News at Ten* and the BBC's *Nine O'Clock News*.

ITN took delivery of its own helicopter in the summer – an Aerospaciale Squirrel – the first British television news organization ever to do so. Helicopters had been used many times before, but always hired. Now with a helicopter on permanent standby at its pad in Denham in Buckinghamshire, a crew could be scrambled at a moment's notice to go anywhere in the country.

And Finally...

With workers on British Rail holding a strike, commuter chaos was expected on the journeys to and from London. But Robin Kingswood was determined to beat the strike and travel, not only in comfort, but certainly with style.

Mr Kingswood owned an amphibious car and planned to beat the traffic by driving down the Thames to work.

1990

FOR YEARS THE WORLD had been waiting for the release from jail of Nelson Mandela, the then leader of the African National Congress. It came in February when Mr Mandela walked out of Victor Verster prison near Cape Town. It was a historic moment. He'd been sentenced, twenty-six years before, to life for sabotage and plotting to overthrow South Africa's apartheid government.

During that long incarceration his image – never mind interviews with him – was banned from publication inside South Africa and he was never photographed or filmed. No one outside his immediate family and friends knew what he looked like. The year before his release *News at Ten* commissioned a local artist to paint Mandela's portrait as he imagined him to be twenty-five years after he was jailed, on the basis of old photographs and extensive interviews with his family and friends. The result, shown exclusively on *News at Ten*, turned out to be a remarkably accurate picture. It didn't stay exclusive for long, though. The African National Congress immediately adopted it for their campaign posters. It was soon, much to the South African government's annoyance, being paraded by thousands of black demonstrators.

This was not ITN's only attempt to get a picture of Mr Mandela before he was released. Two years earlier, he was suddenly taken to hospital from prison in Cape Town. Reporters were barred from the hospital but, on the pretext of visiting a relative and with a camera

Lawrence McGinty reporting underwater in Scapa Flow on the wreck of one of the German navy warships sunk there during the Second World War.

concealed in a bag, ITN's Southern Africa correspondent Kevin Dunn got inside with his six-year-old daughter. Kevin says, 'We worked our way from floor to floor until I spotted the tell-tale security. Blurting out that my daughter urgently needed the toilet, we made off down the corridor only to be stopped by a plain-clothes policeman ten feet from Mr Mandela's room.' When Mr Mandela was subsequently transferred to a clinic, an ITN cameraman checked himself in for medical tests he obviously did not need and spent a day and a night hiding in the toilet hoping, in vain, to catch him on film.

There were many false alarms about Mr Mandela's release before it finally happened. On one occasion

Trevor McDonald meeting Nelson Mandela after the ANC leader had been freed from jail in South Africa.

foreign journalists in Johannesburg received a round-robin pager message saying Mandela was to be freed that afternoon and leaving a contact number which appeared to be from the Bureau of Information in Pretoria. Many hearts skipped a beat, many newsrooms were sent into a frenzy. The panic was such that President de Klerk, holidaying on a beach in the Cape, was himself disturbed by the hoax and had to issue an official denial.

When Mr Mandela was finally released on a Sunday afternoon the pictures were sent live around the world. His first full day of freedom was recorded on *News at Ten* the following day including his first news conference. It was Kevin Dunn who asked him the first question he had taken from a journalist for more

than quarter of a century. Kevin says, 'It wasn't very imaginative. I welcomed him on behalf of the world's press and asked how it felt to be a free man!'

The first interview Mr Mandela gave after his release was to Trevor McDonald. It was a journalistic coup. The reasons behind it were quite practical ones. The ITN team in South Africa had spent quite a lot of time working with the black South African trade union organization – COSATU – which was masterminding the media coverage of Mr Mandela's release. The night before the release, *News at Ten* editor David Mannion had been to see his COSATU contacts to check on the arrangements. They told him they were expecting hundreds of people. David told them they were wrong – it would be thousands, and he offered to draw up a media plan for the next day. By way of thanks they allowed Trevor the first interview.

The world's media was camped outside Mr Mandela's small house in the township of Soweto. There were flat-back lorries being used as platforms by the world's top anchormen, Trevor among them. The South African authorities had taken a lot of persuading to allow ITN to present a live programme from Soweto later that night. It was to be at 10.00pm British time which was midnight in South Africa.

One of the key ingredients of any such programme is an interviewee – someone the presenter can talk to if there is a pause in the proceedings. During the day David Mannion went to see Archbishop Desmond Tutu who had a house very close by in the township – even though he was Archbishop of Cape Town. When he got into the Archbishop's house, there was the man himself dancing round the living room with joy. The Archbishop agreed to be the interviewee. At 11.30pm, the streets of Soweto were crammed with other dancing, happy people. David fought his way through the streets to the Archbishop's house. The next problem was, how could he get him back through the crowds to Trevor's lorry 250 yards away? 'Oh, don't worry about that,' said Archbishop Tutu. As David tried to steer him through the streets the crowds lifted the Archbishop up on to their shoulders – and then lifted David up too. Together they were passed from person to person up to the lorry. Trevor said later that David looked like the great white god of Soweto.

Trevor got a bit of a surprise in January when he was having one of the newscasters' occasional get-togethers over lunch at the White Tower restaurant in London. He was there with colleagues including Sandy Gall, Alastair Burnet, Alastair Stewart and Nicholas Owen. They were all in on the big secret. Trevor was about to appear on *This is Your Life*, with Michael Aspel, although of course Trevor didn't know that.

During the meal, the Thames Television crew making the programme had to be able to get their cameras in

The poll tax riots in March. Police clashed with protesters opposed to the introduction of the new Community Charge which replaced the old system of rates.

place without Trevor seeing. So the doors to the dining room had to be closed. The others had been told that Michael Aspel would appear as a waiter and they were on the edge of their seats waiting. Eventually the door opened and a waiter came through. It was a real one. A few minutes later, the door opened again, and the same waiter came in. This happened several times before Michael Aspel eventually appeared with a glass of brandy. Trevor instantly looked across at Alastair Burnet, presuming he was the object of Michael Aspel's attention. A few hours later it was Trevor who was sitting on the stage in the Thames Television studio.

Fiona Armstrong

Fiona Armstrong studied German at London University, taking a sabbatical in 1979 to edit the student newspaper *Sennet*. Her first job in broadcasting was as a reporter with Radio 210 in Reading. She moved to television in 1982, working for BBC Manchester's *North West Tonight* programme. After three years Fiona went further north to Border Television to present their regional news programme *Lookaround*.

In 1987 Fiona joined ITN and over the next five years presented *News at Ten*, *News at One* and *News at 5.40*. While at ITN she reported on the plight of the children of AIDS victims in Uganda, and covered one of ITN's royal specials: The Prince and Princess of Wales in Western Africa.

Fiona twice made news herself in 1990. In January she was travelling home to Carlisle when her car was in a pile-up with two other cars and a refuse lorry. Despite a whiplash injury, she managed to get out and comfort the terrified children in another car for one and a half hours. In April she suffered burns to her hands and feet in a chip-pan accident.

She left ITN in 1992 to join GMTV as their main female presenter.

In 1994 Fiona returned to Border TV to present three half-hour programmes on her favourite pastime, entitled *Fiona on Fly-Fishing*. She has written two books, *F is for Fly-Fishing* (a reference to the controversial 'F for fanciability factor', which GMTV used to launch their breakfast programme), and *The Commuter's Cookbook*.

Fiona has also worked as a newsreader for BBC World Television and an occasional presenter for BBC Radio 2 as well as reporting for ITV's daily show *This Morning*.

Fiona Armstrong preparing to read the news.

Alastair Burnet found himself in the news when he had a fall and suffered some nasty cuts to his famous face. Photos of Alastair with a plaster on his forehead appeared in some of the newspapers. He told them later it was nothing to do with his fondness for an occasional whisky. 'I'm always drinking. This was just a minor falling over.' The accident happened after work one night. He was admitted to hospital but discharged himself the next morning. He wanted to come back to work but his ITN friends persuaded him to stay out of the limelight until he felt a bit better. They took him to the Berners Hotel near ITN House. Only four people knew he was there. Alastair thought perhaps the press had found out where he was because the phone kept ringing and a woman's voice asked to speak to him. Assured it couldn't be a reporter, Alastair then did answer the phone the next time it rang. He was then heard to say, 'Hello Prime Minister. Yes, thank you, I'm fine.'

Trevor McDonald joined the *News at Ten* team of newscasters on a permanent basis – as speculation began to increase about who might take over the top

spot from Alastair Burnet when he eventually retired. The three in the running were Trevor, Julia and Alastair Stewart. ITN denied there were any plans for Alastair Burnet to hang up his earpiece.

ITN crews are used to security checks as they go about their work but one crew was rather surprised that there weren't any at, of all things, the London Security Conference. The guest speakers were the Foreign Office Minister William Waldegrave and the Metropolitan Police Commissioner Sir Peter Imbert. Cameraman Neil Hamilton and soundman Patrick Hilliard set up their equipment inside the hall. Another soundman there was banging the metal lectern on the stage, trying to move the top. He was obviously having problems because something was stuck in its way. He called out to Patrick, 'Have you put anything inside this lectern?' Patrick said he hadn't and the other soundman carried on banging down on the lectern. Once they'd set up their gear, Neil and Patrick were asked to leave the hall so the

John Suchet escorting the new Prime Minister, John Major, around ITN's new building in central London.

sniffer dogs could check it. The crew knew something was wrong when the police ordered everyone out of the building. They realized it was a bomb scare but they needed to retrieve their equipment. Neil managed to get back inside and could then film what was going on. They found out later that the reason the lectern had jammed was because inside it was a lunchbox containing four pounds of explosives.

For ITN's award-winning cameraman Eugene Campbell, 1990 was to be quite a year. At the start of it he and reporter Peter Sharp brought to the world's attention one of the worst legacies of the dark days of the Ceausescu regime – Romania's system of orphanages. Their story started – as many do on *News at Ten* – with a newspaper cutting that Peter was asked to check out. Diplomats knew there were lots of orphanages around the capital, Bucharest. The children in those were generally healthy. What no one really knew about was that there were other orphanages where children with handicaps were left by parents who didn't want them.

With the help of a local television technician who lived in the city, Eugene and Peter found an orphanage which showed just how sinister the Ceausescu regime had been. It housed 700 children under three years old. At first they were shown the healthy and relatively happy orphans. After some persuasion, they were allowed to film a very different group of children within the same building but kept separate from the first group. They were mentally or physically handicapped. What Eugene noticed first was that none of this second group of children cried. It was as though they could cry no more. They ran up to Eugene and Peter and put their arms round their legs, saying, 'Mamma, Mamma.' When Peter's report was transmitted in Britain it caused an outcry. It also provoked hundreds of calls from viewers, not just asking what they could do to help but offering to adopt the handicapped children.

Eugene's next big story of the year was the poll tax riots in London. It felt like quite a familiar assignment for a cameraman who was born in and worked in Northern Ireland. When the protests

Unwanted children in Romanian state orphanages. Peter Sharp highlighted their plight and began an international campaign for would-be parents to adopt them.

The first pictures of Iraq's invasion of Kuwait, shot by an amateur cameramen, were broadcast on ITN. They showed the sky line of Kuwait City with the Emir's palace engulfed in smoke in the distance (top) and the Iraqi armoured personnel carriers in the streets of Kuwait City (above).

broke out in Whitehall they caught the police completely unaware. They were too busy trying to control the situation to worry about keeping Eugene at a distance from the fighting. The rioters were using anything they could get their hands on. Eugene was hit by a traffic cone. Then he had to jump in the air as a spade came flying towards him at knee height. He got separated from Anne Leuchars who was the reporter on the story. As the riots were coming to an end Eugene was grabbed by the friends of a man who had been hit badly on the

head. They wanted him to be filmed. Eugene ended up with the man's blood on him. When he was finally reunited with the ITN team they thought Eugene himself had been injured.

The third big assignment – on board American warships in the Gulf – began in October. It ended up being by far the most dangerous. Saddam Hussein had invaded Kuwait in August. The Western allies were sending ships and troops into the Gulf ready to attack Saddam if he didn't withdraw from Kuwait.

Eugene was working with reporter Michael Nicholson. Other crews had been given permission to follow the Army and Air Force. A naval contact had given them permission to film with the Royal Navy. Initially Eugene was on the command ship HMS *London* but when the conflict began at the start of 1991 he moved to HMS *Gloucester* which was a front line air defence destroyer.

He and Michael each had to live in long cupboards. That sounds bad enough. Eventually they had to share them with sailors on board. Sometimes the alarm signifying 'Action Stations' would sound. That was the highest state of alert, suggesting they might be attacked at any moment. Eugene, Michael and the ship's crew had to put on their flak jackets and protective clothes and go to the bridge. There were fifteen 'Action Stations' during the six weeks of the war. Eugene says it still makes him go cold when he sees the film he took during those frightening moments. Relations with the ship's Lynx helicopter crews became so good that the flight commander would take Eugene on search and destroy missions in place of one of their missiles – sitting in the aircraft of course, not strapped underneath!

It was on such a mission that Eugene's most frightening moment came. The day had begun as normal with breakfast and Eugene and the helicopter's pilot and navigator were then given their packed lunches in brown paper bags.

Their flight that morning was along the Kuwaiti coastline – flying about a mile and a half away from it. That was supposed to be out of range of the Iraqi surface-to-air missiles. The helicopter crew had been given a geographic square of sea to 'sweep' for Iraqi warships and they found one. The pilot called in to the American command ship to be given clearance to attack the Iraqi warship – an order known as 'weapons free'. The crew heard the reply: 'Roger, Weapons free.' The helicopter then had to sit and hover while its radar locked onto the Iraqi ship. The Sea Skua missiles that the Lynx used initially face towards the helicopter once they are fired so they can carry on taking radar information as they head towards their target. Halfway through their trajectory they flip over and point towards the target. The significance of this is that the helicopter has to remain in exactly the same place in the air for half the missile's flight, making the helicopter itself a sitting target for – on this occasion – the Iraqi warship's 76-millimetre anti-aircraft guns.

The Lynx wasn't hit and Eugene and the crew saw the missile blow the Iraqi ship's superstructure off, almost certainly sinking it. The helicopter turned rapidly back to base. It had been a highly charged and shocking experience, but Eugene remembers the amazing contrast with ordinary life as he and the crew ate their packed lunches of cheese and crackers on the flight back. The next day he and the crewmen went back to the same stretch of water and saw the submerged warship surrounded by life-rafts and life-jackets. Almost certainly everyone on board had been killed.

ITN moved into its new home, 200 Gray's Inn Road, towards the end of the year. For a time, ITN was broadcasting out of both old and new buildings at the same time as the programmes were relocated one by one. The new headquarters were to win the best corporate building award and its design found its way on to architecture syllabuses in universities around the world. But for four years it was to be a financial millstone round the company's neck.

And Finally...

After years of dutiful service, Liverpool policeman Frank Grunnill retired. As always, his colleagues wanted to give him a present. But they did not choose a gold watch or any of the usual gifts. They gave him a horse.

PC Grunnill served as a mounted policeman and it seemed only right that he was given his horse, Vindicator, as a leaving present.

Vindicator was eighteen years old, making him the oldest police horse in Britain and a veteran of several Grand Nationals – not as a runner but as an escort to the winner after the race to the winner's enclosure.

1991

T HE YEAR BEGAN with the Gulf War –
Operation Desert Storm – after Iraq's President
Saddam Hussein invaded Kuwait in August the
previous year. Unlike the invasion which no one had
expected, the first attack by the allies came more or
less on schedule. The Western Allies had given
Saddam Hussein until 15 January to pull out of
Kuwait or else they would attack. On 16 January that
attack was launched.

ITN's editor Stewart Purvis was talking to Middle East
correspondent Brent Sadler in Baghdad on a special
sound circuit which belonged to the American news
network CNN, in the early hours of the morning
Baghdad time. They were discussing Brent's safety and
that of his crew when suddenly CNN asked to have the

**The head of the Allied Forces in the Gulf, American General
'Stormin'' Norman Schwarzkopf.**

The USS *Wisconsin* opening fire in the Gulf.

circuit back. The bombing had begun. ITN broke into
Midweek Sports Special on ITV at 11.47pm and seven
hours later ITN was still broadcasting. It became an
immensely draining time for those in the field and
those in the newsroom. ITN was broadcasting longer
programmes and more programmes – a Gulf update
at 8.00pm in the evening became a regular part of the
ITV schedule, as did long programmes in the night.
Tired bodies could be found asleep in corridors of the
new building as ITN tried to meet the demand from
viewers for information.

Brent Sadler was one of the first reporters to get into
Baghdad at the start of the Gulf crisis. To fly in from
Jordan, where he and his team had been waiting,
they had to hire a 300-seat plane which Brent had
to pay for in cash – the cost: $25,000.

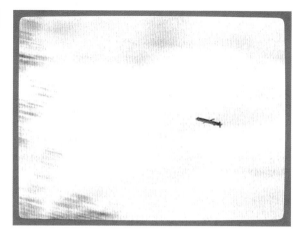

They landed in an empty airport because no one else would fly in. The Iraqis who were assigned to look after them took them to their hotel – the Hilton. On the way Brent said he'd like to call in at the British Embassy. Nothing had been heard of the ambassador or his staff for some time. Brent wasn't sure what to expect. When they got there everyone was playing cricket! Brent stayed in Baghdad when the allies

The ITN team in Saudi Arabia playing Scrabble to pass the time during another Scud missile alert.

Brent Sadler (above left) turning during a report to watch a cruise missile (above) flying over Baghdad.

began to attack the city. It was a difficult decision for Brent and editors back in London to make for safety reasons. Brent wanted to stay. There was an amazing story to tell. One of the key chapters of it was when he and his crew filmed Cruise missiles flying over Baghdad. No television audience had ever seen anything like it before. Brent described it perfectly with a phrase that has become part of ITN

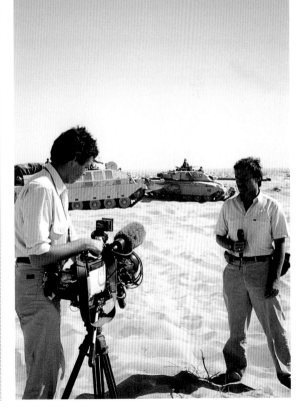

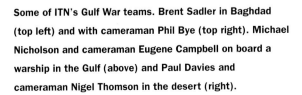

Some of ITN's Gulf War teams. Brent Sadler in Baghdad (top left) and with cameraman Phil Bye (top right). Michael Nicholson and cameraman Eugene Campbell on board a warship in the Gulf (above) and Paul Davies and cameraman Nigel Thomson in the desert (right).

folklore. The missiles with their incredible guidance systems were, he said, 'map-reading themselves' along Iraqi motorways.

When the war proper started, those in Baghdad weren't the only ones who had to take care. Because of the threat of reprisal attacks, the team in Saudi Arabia had to wear chemical, biological and nuclear suits and carry gas masks at all times. The gas mask holders made handy places to keep notebooks and pens as well! Iraq started firing Scud missiles at its neighbours, Israel and Saudi Arabia, once the allied air attacks began. Every time there was an alert, the ITN team in Saudi Arabia had to go into the air raid shelters. They became rather blasé about it, until an American base took a direct hit. To pass the time Alastair Stewart and his colleagues got to play rather a lot of Scrabble. But they had to wear their gas masks. No one could have a drink to relax from the tension because of the Saudi ban on alcohol. They

Alastair Stewart headed ITN's team of reporters, cameramen, producers, picture editors and engineers in the Gulf.

had three 'dry' months, apart from the time when a friend from the American Network CNN was able to smuggle a small bottle of whisky, which was very gratefully received. It was only when the ITN team returned to London after the war was over that they found – in a false bottom of one of their equipment boxes – there was a stash of whisky and gin. It had been sent over to raise spirits during the fighting but no one had known it was there.

One of *News at Ten*'s greatest triumphs of the war came once the allies had liberated Kuwait from the Iraqis. Throughout the war most reporters were assigned to the British forces, including ITN's. But Alastair Stewart was able to travel into Kuwait with the liberating Saudi army. When they got to Kuwait they were welcomed by cheering Kuwaitis who, once or twice, almost overran Alastair during his live reports. One other reporter who managed to slip the leash a little was Peter Sharp. He was sent to Khafji on the coast of Saudi Arabia – a town of around 90,000 people on the border with Kuwait. It was now totally deserted. He and his crew set up in an abandoned hotel. At the start of the air attacks they were able to film the RAF Harriers on their bombing raids against Iraqi positions in Kuwait.

One day Peter thought he could smell petrol and assumed it was coming from the crew's generator. Shortly afterwards he saw a cormorant covered in oil. He put two and two together and came up with a story that no one had foreseen. Iraq had attacked Kuwait's oil installations and left them pouring thousands of gallons of oil into the sea. As Peter says, 'The sea didn't splash on the beaches, it gurgled.' They filmed the story and then worked overnight to get it finished. Peter remembers being asleep in the afternoon and waking up to see United States President George Bush on CNN. He was talking about the pictures in Peter's report that they had transmitted to London only twenty minutes earlier. Mr Bush called what the Iraqis were doing 'environmental terrorism'.

This report had alerted the world to what was going on. It also alerted Saudi police to Peter's presence on the border and soon he was taken back to Dhahran. That probably saved Peter's life. That night Iraqi troops streamed over the border from Kuwait and captured Khafji.

When the Gulf war finally ended there was at last a breathing space for the Queen to come and officially open ITN's new building. She was escorted round the newsroom by *News at Ten* editor David Mannion. He had been told he must call her 'Mam' and not 'Ma'am'. In case he forgot, he was told to think of the word 'Spam' as it rhymes with 'Mam'. As David says, 'Someone said you'll end up calling her your Royal Luncheon Meat!'

Peter Sharp reporting on a tank battle during the Gulf War (top). He also reported on the environmental damage from the pollution caused by Iraqi attacks on Kuwaiti oil fields (above).

The new building in Gray's Inn Road had cost £120 million to build and, by the time all the staff had moved in, about £45 million to equip. During the year a big accounting error had been discovered in ITN's budget – it meant a black hole in its accounts. At the same time, ITN had to cut costs, partly to secure a new contract with ITV: 135 staff were made redundant including some *News at Ten* reporters – sports correspondent Giles Smith and home affairs correspondent Sarah Cullen. Other older faces, Desmond Hamill and Keith Hatfield, took voluntary redundancy or early retirement.

ITN Chairman David Nicholas greeting the Queen (above) on her visit to open ITN's new headquarters (below).

Amid the financial difficulties that summer the two knights of *News at Ten* – Sir Alastair Burnet and Sir David Nicholas, by now the company's chairman – both announced they would be retiring. Alastair was the public face of *News at Ten*. David had been for many years its unseen driving force. They had been colleagues, friends and, together, architects of *News at Ten* since those first pioneering days.

The break-up of what had been called Yugoslavia became a bloody three-sided war. Like any war zone it had real dangers for camera crews and this was brought home to everyone on *News at Ten* when reporter David Chater was shot in the back by a sniper's dum-dum bullet when he went to Vukovar in Croatia – the scene of some of the worst fighting of the war. He was wearing a flak jacket but it didn't stop the bullet. The bullet destroyed one of his kidneys, damaged his intestines and left him with a cavity in his stomach. David said, 'It was like being cut in two by a mortar. I remember hearing gunfire and then falling. I fought to stay awake for fear of never waking up again. There were five minutes of total shock. Everything started to shut down. My hearing went and my vision clouded over. Then suddenly my senses came back and with them searing pain.'

He and his crew had taken refuge from the battle in a wrecked church as Serbian tanks rumbled past. David had arrived in Croatia only the previous day. That night's *News at Ten* showed what happened. David was shown saying with a smile, 'They haven't got our range, have they?' as the firing started. Moments later he was on the ground. His crew helped get him to

hospital by helicopter where he spent three days in intensive care. He needed eighteen pints of blood and a five-hour operation. After that, he was flown back to Britain and spent another week in hospital in London. David had covered wars before. 'You never *ever* think it is going to happen you,' he said. Vukovar, where David was shot, was under siege for six weeks. This beautiful town on the banks of the Duna River had the misfortune of being largely Croatian and being right on the border with the Serb Republic.

During those six weeks the mainly Serbian Yugoslav Army pounded it with their tanks and field artillery until barely one brick stood on top of another. The entire town was reduced to rubble. When the cease-fire finally came and the residents were able to climb out of their cellars and leave the smouldering wreckage, Michael Nicholson and his crew were the first to reach the hospital. Like everywhere else, it was completely destroyed, but down in the basement they discovered a vision of hell. Hundreds of people were crowded in among the heating pipes and boilers, some of them two or three to a bed and, in the thick of it all, the doctors were still working. The doctors were cramped so tightly that they had to perform operations wherever they could, often with

Reporter David Chater was badly wounded by a stray bullet in Vukovar, Croatia.

A Serbian sniper picking out his target in Croatia.

no anaesthetic nor adequate dressings. All the sheets had long since been used up.

One surgeon, a young woman who spoke perfect English, said that she hadn't been above ground for three weeks even though she lived only across the street. She laughed and added, 'I hope my house is still there.' Cameraman Phil Bye remembers, 'We didn't have the heart to say it almost certainly wasn't.' She took them around her improvised ward and there they found Sanja. She'd just been born when the bombardment started and her family had sheltered in the vaults of a factory with hundreds of others. The cellar was brick-built and they would have been safe there but an artillery shell had burst in through the only vulnerable point – an air vent. Sanja's grand-mother, who was holding her at the time, was killed outright. Sanja received abdominal injuries. The doctors had given their own blood to keep her alive. Somehow, they said, she had become the focus of their hope. If she survived then they all would.

When Michael's report was shown on *News at Ten*, Sanja suddenly became the focus for the programme's viewers too. For weeks they had seen pictures of close combat and destroyed buildings, but suddenly the plight of this child brought it home to people what the war was about. The ITN phone lines were jammed

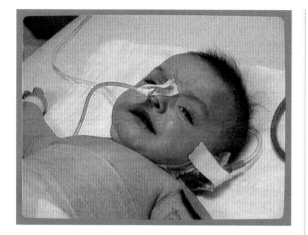

Sanja – a young victim of the civil war in Vukovar, Croatia (top) and as a lively seven-year old in 1998 (above).

after the programme with people calling to find out what happened to baby Sanja. The next day Michael and Phil went back to Vukovar and returned to the hospital. In the meantime, since they were last there, the Serbs had taken it over. They were told later that all the wounded men of fighting age were taken away separately, almost certainly to be killed.

What was probably their mass grave was discovered some years later. The Serbs said Sanja and the other women and children had been taken to Serb hospitals. The ITN crew spent a day following trail after false trail until the evening when they finally found Sanja and her mother in a hospital in Belgrade. She was, the doctors said, very sick, but they were

sure she would survive. Sanja's mother looked exhausted and somewhat uncomfortable. After all, this was in fact the military hospital and some of the patients had been involved in the destruction of her town. Ironically she, herself, was a Serb.

Some years later, as *News at Ten* often did, the crew went back to Vukovar with Sanja and her family. The town is slowly starting to recover with some rebuilding going on, but their house will never be habitable. Sanja's parents, reunited after the war, still have something to live for. Their daughter – now a lively seven-year-old – skipped and played in the ruins.

The beautiful port city of Dubrovnik on the Adriatic coast of Croatia was perhaps best known as a holiday resort, until the civil war in the former Yugoslavia. In October it came under attack from the big guns of the Serb-dominated Yugoslav army that threatened at one stage to reduce its historic buildings to rubble. Paul Davies was sent to cover the story. The Yugoslav forces were preventing journalists from getting to Dubrovnik but Paul heard that a protest flotilla of some of the former Yugoslavia's leading singers, actors and playwrights was going to sail there from the port of Split. Paul got a message to them, asking them to delay their departure time until he and his crew could join them. They agreed, welcoming the chance for a European television crew to publicize their protest. Boxes containing edit kits, cameras and other equipment were duly transferred on to the lead boat in rather choppy waters.

At one point the Yugoslav navy did intercept the lead boat, the *Slavia*, and the dozens of little fishing boats that were following and threatened to sink them. The protesters called their bluff and sailed on. They sailed into Dubrovnik to a hero's welcome. Paul describes being in Dubrovnik like this: 'It felt like we had strayed onto a film set where the director had somehow mixed up the chapters of his history book. Russian-made wire-guided missiles were crashing into Dubrovnik's medieval walls. Federal navy frigates, tanks and heavy artillery were pouring shells into ramparts that were built to keep out arrows and spears.'

The Croatian army were like no other force. Many spoke excellent English – not surprising because most had been employed in the tourist industry before the siege began.

Along with the rest of the city Paul spent four days pinned down by the non-stop bombardment of the Serb-led Yugoslav forces. Thousands of shells were falling on the city. On one day Paul decided to count the bangs. At 8.00am in the morning he gave up at 200. On another day he was blown off his feet and very nearly over the ramparts of the harbour wall when a shell landed nearby. His cameraman, Nigel Thomson, took even more risks. He climbed on to the wall as the port came under attack from land and sea while everyone else was huddled in cellars.

Getting the pictures was dangerous work. Getting reports back to London was difficult too. At first Paul could transmit from the local television station until the Yugoslav airforce bombed the transmitter. Then reports were put on powerboats which would transport wounded people out of the city and then return carrying more ammunition and supplies. When the Yugoslav navy sank two of the powerboats, there was then no other way of getting the reports out. It was during this time that Paul and picture editor Fred Hickey hit on the idea of creating a television diary of the siege of Dubrovnik – a day-by-day record of the destruction of the city.

Once it was finished there was still the problem of how to get it back to London. The Yugoslav forces allowed a short ceasefire to allow women, children and some foreign nationals to leave the city. The ITN team took the opportunity to partially disband with the hope that one of those leaving would be able to

Nigel Thomson filming the siege of Dubrovnik on its historic city wall.

get a tape back to London. Several copies of the 'Diary of a Siege' were made. One was hidden in a box of equipment. The videotape of another was unlaced from its cassette and wrapped around a bandage with sticking tape on the outside to disguise it. Another was placed in the shoe of a producer. Several were secreted around the ferry. Paul remembers one in particular being sealed inside a plastic bag and submerged in an oil can in the engine room. As Paul says, many are still probably ploughing their way up and down the Adriatic. In the end it was one of the less sophisticated attempts at smuggling out the video diary that made it to London.

Paul's award-winning report 'Dubrovnik – Diary of a Siege' occupied the first half of *News at Ten* one night. The highlight for Paul was that when his report was beamed around the world there was massive international pressure on the Yugoslav President Slobodan Milosevic to call off the bombardment. Paul says now, 'It would be nice to think that with a little help from us, Dubrovnik survived.'

Paul and his ITN team have a permanent invitation to return to Dubrovnik from its people. He did go back once at the end of a long and difficult assignment in

Extract from 'Diary of a Siege', 14 November 1991

It was early Saturday morning when the battle for Dubrovnik intensified: tanks and heavy guns of the Serb-dominated federal army pouring in fire from their positions in the surrounding mountains.

The majority of the city's population took to the underground shelters. But those who ventured outside witnessed a co-ordinated land, sea and air attack on their city. Once again the main target for the federal army guns was the Napoleonic fort above Dubrovnik: the Croatian defenders' most vital position. Federal navy ships appeared offshore to join the attack.

Shells falling into Dubrovnik's main harbour hit one of the ferries which had been unable to leave port because of the naval blockade. It was now impossible for the thousands trapped here to escape the bombardment. In Dubrovnik hospital most of the casualties were suffering from wounds caused by flying shrapnel. Doctors say more than half the victims treated here have been civilians.

Sunday morning in Dubrovnik's gothic cathedral, they prayed for peace. For many of the congregation this was the first time in days they'd dared to venture out of the bomb shelters.

One exploded through the roof of a house built four centuries ago. In all, four mortars fell inside the city walls that day, shrapnel exploding into the convent. The tranquillity of the fourteenth-century Franciscan monastery was also shattered. As the federal troops closed in, the few residents left on the streets took what cover they could. This woman had risked her life to rescue her dog from its kennel in the old harbour.

Monday and Dubrovnik's main street is deserted in preparation for the inevitable resumption of this one-sided battle.

Residential areas devastated, with shells falling closer and closer to the old city, for the first time striking its medieval walls. Down the centuries, Dubrovnik's citizens have defied would-be invaders, now their old ramparts faced twentieth-century war machines.

But at least the walls offered some protection - outside there was no escape. Tuesday morning and the attack everyone had feared but most secretly believed could never happen: a deliberate and sustained assault on the old city. This was not a case of shells going astray - it was a calculated decision to irreparably damage a city that

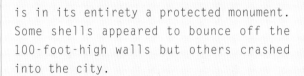

Paul Davies reports from the seige of Dubrovnik.

is in its entirety a protected monument. Some shells appeared to bounce off the 100-foot-high walls but others crashed into the city.

The federal army was now using Soviet-made wire-guided missiles against walls first built to keep out arrows and spears. Missiles landing in the old port set boats and buildings ablaze. In the hotel bar scenes reminiscent of London's East End during the Blitz: the locals singing traditional songs to drown the noise of the guns.

The city they called the Pearl of the Adriatic – its history and its beauty attracted tourists from around the world. Now its ancient structures are lit up by flames while its citizens await the next onslaught.

Wednesday and Thursday the fires still burnt but at least a respite from the fighting, only now there was another agony. A cease-fire brokered by the EC observers allowed the evacuation of women, children and the wounded but only sixteen hundred could go. On the dockside they queued, waiting to see who would be allowed to board the ferry and who had to stay. Families separated, no way of knowing when they would see their homes again or how many of the husbands and sons left behind would survive.

Paul Davies, *News at Ten*, Dubrovnik.

Margaret Thatcher wiped away a tear during an interview with Michael Brunson as she remembered how she was forced to step down as Prime Minister.

Bosnia. As he walked into the reception of the Hotel Argentina where he'd stayed, the receptionist looked up and said, 'Welcome home.'

News at Ten's Moscow correspondents Tim Ewart and Penny Marshall were married that summer and certainly didn't think there'd be such a big story on their 'patch' while they were on honeymoon. They were happy to leave the bureau in the hands of a junior reporter called Robert Moore, and told the foreign desk at ITN they didn't wanted to be disturbed on the island of Jumby Bay, off the coast of Antigua. They were actually in bed when ITN finally tracked them down to tell them that there had been a coup against President Gorbachev. Mr Gorbachev had also been enjoying a holiday – in the Crimea rather than the Caribbean. Hardline communists, including Gorbachev's own vice-president, who didn't like the direction of the Soviet President's reforms cut the phone lines at his holiday retreat and placed him under house arrest.

He owed his political survival to his political rival, Boris Yeltsin, the President of the Russian Republic. Mr Yeltsin publicly opposed the communist coup by climbing on top of a tank outside the Russian Parliament. Thousands of

Muscovites took to the streets to support Yeltsin. It was a big story by any standards, but very few ITN reporters had visas to report from the Soviet Union. Tim and Penny of course did. The race was on to get them back to Moscow. They had to make a tortuous journey via Puerto Rico and Frankfurt to get back to the Moscow bureau. So much for not being disturbed. (That fledgling reporter in the Moscow bureau, by the way, is now ITN's diplomatic editor.)

ITN's political editor Michael Brunson got the first television interview with Mrs Thatcher since she'd stood down as Prime Minister and left Downing Street the year before. She was still very emotional about the way she had been forced out of office and cried during the interview as she remembered how, one by one, the Cabinet told her she should go.

And Finally...

With Christmas drawing closer, Bristol police expected the usual increase in shoplifting. So they came up with an unusual way of alerting shoppers to crime in the high street... plastic policemen.

At 6 feet 7 inches tall and costing £95 each, the cut-out coppers were to be positioned in shopping precincts. Police were quick to state that although they needed more real policemen the images were not there to replace humans, they were a crime prevention initiative.

1992

OF COURSE THE BIGGEST change to *News at Ten* was that, for the first time in its twenty-five-year history, the programme would be presented by just one person: Trevor McDonald – then as now voted Britain's most popular newscaster in opinion polls. Research had suggested that the viewers were slightly bemused by the roundabout of different faces in different combinations presenting the programme. Also research was done in the United States on how television news viewers there relate to a sole 'anchor', to use the American jargon. Viewers, it was thought, now wanted continuity – a face they could recognize – if they

Trevor McDonald on location in South Africa, preparing for a live report.

weren't to be seduced into hopping to one of the other channels.

Also, the reasons for having two newscasters were now long gone. A double-headed approach was a big advantage in the days of film, before live reports were so common, and before computerized graphics. You needed to be able to bounce stories from one to the other to get a certain amount of variety. Now you just needed one person – standing on the bridge – co-ordinating the world's news. The editor of *News at Ten* at the time, David Mannion remembers how the news was broken to Trevor that he was to be the sole presenter. 'I said, "Trevor, I've got some good news and some bad news. The good news is you've got the job. The bad news is you're not going to have any social life for five nights of the week."'

The idea of continuity was also applied more rigorously than ever to *News at Ten* reporters. Viewers wanted to see the same 'family' of faces telling them what had been going on that day – people who they felt they could trust – rather than a succession of different faces who came and went and sometimes weren't seen on the 'flagship' programme for days or even weeks. The bongs would be staying but the set would be changing. The backdrop of the night-time skyline of London was replaced with a new high-tech set with television screens over Trevor's shoulder. *News at Ten* has always prided itself on its ability to react faster than the competition to breaking news stories but, in the same way that

Trevor McDonald, confirmed as the sole presenter of *News at Ten*, on the new-look set.

viewers responded to familiar faces, the new thinking was they liked the programme to have a familiar feel. So a special report was introduced every night – a slightly longer and even more carefully crafted piece – that would run in the middle of part two. It would usually be preceded by a 'wrap' of three shorter film items, read by Trevor, to vary the look and pace of the programme. Sport would occupy a regular place in the programme and so would that *News at Ten* trademark – the 'And Finally'. The theme music was rearranged for the first time since 1967.

Once again Big Ben would still be part of the opening titles – but there was nearly a calamity when those titles were being made. Part of the Houses of Parliament almost got demolished. ITN had hired a balloon from a company in Vienna from which to

film the Big Ben sequence. It had been windy for three days and the balloon had to go back after four – so on the final night it was a matter of now or never. Because of the wind, the balloon was on the end of a rope. The rope was anchored in the parliamentary grounds. All seemed to be going well until a gust of wind blew the balloon towards one of the small towers on the top of the building and the rope got caught around the tower. If there had then been another strong gust, the tower would have been pulled over. Somehow the next gust untangled the rope and the balloon blew clear of the danger zone. Despite the let-off, it is a night many who were there remember every time they see the start of *News at Ten* – because of what might have been.

A rather odd piece of television history was made in January, involving the Northern Ireland Secretary Peter Brooke. He caused outrage one night when he appeared on an Irish television chat show, singing

'My Darling Clementine', shortly after a terrorist attack. Many people thought he was insensitive. Just before the musical part of his interview, *News at Ten* arranged a live link-up with *The Gay Byrne Show*. During his conversation with Mr Brooke, the host paused and said to his studio audience, 'Excuse us one moment, while Mr Brooke talks to *News at Ten* in London.' It must have made very strange viewing for people watching in the Irish Republic.

By the summer the civil war in what was Yugoslavia had been raging for a year. Michael Nicholson had been reporting from Sarajevo when he visited an orphanage. Michael of course has been in many war zones and seen more suffering than perhaps anyone should see. But his journalistic detachment slipped when he saw the plight of the children there. He wanted to do more than report – he wanted to do something to help. One particular child held his attention. She was a nine-year-old girl called Natasha Mihaljcic. When they were filming, Natasha had been the first to follow the crew around. Michael said, 'She was always a child that shone out, always lively and bright and good at looking after the little ones.' She was one of a group of eighty orphans who were to be moved out of Sarajevo because it was so dangerous. They were to be taken to the coastal town of Split and then on to France and Italy until the fighting was over. A relief worker at the orphanage asked him if he would be able to take a child back with him. Michael said, 'I had been doing all these stories from Sarajevo imploring people to be concerned about what is happening there and to do something about it. I decided to do something about it. When I was asked if I could take a child I said I would take Natasha.'

He wrote her name in his passport in the hope that she would be allowed into Britain on his passport. At immigration control at Heathrow, he told inspectors what he had done and who Natasha was. They let them both through. He took her home with him to his house in Surrey – though kept her presence there

Natasha Mihaljcic in her orphanage in Sarajevo (top) before she was brought out of Bosnia by Michael Nicholson (middle). Michael added Natasha to his own passport to get her through British immigration control at Heathrow airport (bottom).

quiet so she had a little time to get used to her very new and very different life.

When she arrived she closed the curtains, as she had done in Sarajevo, because of the fear of flying glass from shells and bullets. She also brought the discipline of her orphanage life with her. She made her own bed, put her clothes away, and washed the dishes after meals. She learned to speak English and to play cricket with Michael and his two grown-up sons. Michael always intended to take her back to Sarajevo when the fighting finished. A few months later, after finding out more about Natasha, the Nicholsons began making plans to adopt her. Natasha's young mother, Milicia, had left her in an orphanage when she was a month old. Her mother, it seems, did come back to collect her when she was three years old but, when social workers found Natasha had been beaten and burnt, they took her back to the orphanage. Her mother saw her three times in eight years. Michael met her when she came to sign the adoption papers. She said she loved her daughter but admitted she had been a bad mother and eventually agreed to sign the papers.

Later, Michael's book, *Natasha's Story*, was made into a film called *Welcome to Sarajevo*. Michael was played by Stephen Dillane. The film was given added realism by use of ITN pictures filmed in Sarajevo.

Back in Bosnia, *News at Ten* reporter Penny Marshall and her crew were to make a discovery that was to change the course of the war. ITN had been promised by the Bosnian Serb leader Radovan Karadzic that their teams could look round the camps where Bosnian men were being held. At the first camp visited by Penny and her colleague Ian Williams from *Channel Four News*, at Omarska, they found hundreds of men in a detention camp, too afraid to talk. At the second, Trnopolje, they filmed young Bosnian Muslim men who had been starved during their detention. The images in Penny's report which occupied most of

the first half of *News at Ten* that night were harrowing. Penny's report helped persuade American President George Bush that some kind of Western military action was now needed – the world could not stand by and watch.

Still in Bosnia, cameraman Nigel Thomson and sound recordist Jim Dutton were hit in a Sarajevo mortar attack. They were filming a Serbian attack on a refugee hotel. Jim's injuries – to his hand – were the more serious. His fingers had to be rebuilt. Nigel (husband of Carol Barnes) got a broken arm. It was the second time he'd been injured that year. He'd been hit by shrapnel in Afghanistan four months earlier.

Also in danger – though in a medical rather than a military sense – was Julia Somerville who had, unknown to most of her *News at Ten* colleagues, collapsed from a brain tumour while she was on holiday in Devon. It was a benign tumour, the size of an orange, which had been spreading around her optic nerves. The delicate operation to remove it lasted nine hours and went according to plan. There was no lasting damage to her sight or to other parts

The Windsor Castle fire in November. It began in the chapel and spread to the castle causing millions of pounds worth of damage. Prince Andrew helped in the rescue of valuable paintings and works of art.

ITN's Penny Marshall and Ian Williams gained exclusive access to a detention camp in Bosnia where Serbs kept Muslim men in terrible conditions.

of her brain. When she was eventually well enough to return to work, only twelve weeks later, the only short-term damage on view was to her hair. She'd had to have it cut off for the operation and not surprisingly it took a little while to grow back. She returned to be greeted by Trevor with a kiss and a bunch of flowers. 'I'm delighted to be back,' she said. 'I feel great, I really do. Coming back to work is a boost – it's the icing on the cake.'

Not long after Julia appeared again on *News at Ten*, Alastair Stewart announced he was leaving to present a new local evening news programme in London for Carlton Television, called *London Tonight*. He had been disappointed when Trevor was made the sole 'anchor' but said he was leaving on friendly terms.

Since then of course he has also gone on to extend his portfolio of presenting to *Police, Camera Action*, on ITV plus his own interview programme on GMTV, *The Sunday Programme*.

Coverage of the General Election campaign threw up an interesting moment of television news. Reporter

Liberal Democrat leader Paddy Ashdown playing a joke on reporter Libby Wiener during a live election report.

Libby Wiener had been assigned to follow the Liberal Democrat leader Paddy Ashdown in the run-up to polling day. She was standing outside a building where Mr Ashdown had been holding a meeting when the man himself appeared behind her during her live report. After a short conversation about what had been going on inside Mr Ashdown said, 'We knew we wouldn't faze you. It's a joke from them in there, you realize that don't you?'

And Finally...

When shepherd Peter Bell left home to start his day he took with him the usual tools of his trade: a shepherd's crook and his faithful dog. But when Peter went off to check on his sheep he didn't use a car, he used a microlite aircraft, carrying his dog, Chips, with him. The airborne sheepdog was quite comfortable overlooking the flocks and, when Peter spotted something and landed, Chips was off and running.

So no matter what the weather, Peter and Chips were the shepherds who watched their flocks by flight.

The Bosnian Camps, 6 August 1992

The Bosnian Serbs don't call Omarska a concentration camp. 'Come in,' they challenged ITN, 'and see it for yourselves.' Under Serbian armed guard for our protection, a three-day journey ended here, at the gates of a disused mine in northern Bosnia.

Here we were shown only several hundred of the two thousand five hundred prisoners - all Muslim men - at Omarska we were told were to be interrogated. Those found guilty of fighting Serbs were then sent to prisoner of war camps, the innocents to refugee camps.

This is all we saw of the prisoners and of Omarska itself. They never spoke. The only voices, those of the guards ordering them to eat faster and leave.

'How are you treated? What are the conditions?' I asked.

'I don't want to tell lies. I can't speak the truth. Thank you for coming.'

And then the men left, back to wherever they had come from, away from our cameras and questions, hidden from the United Nations and the Red Cross - who have been denied access to Omarska - hidden until now from the world.

And so we left, our host fulfilling the promise to show us the second camp, Trnopolje, where two thousand refugees are living. We were not prepared for what we saw and heard there.

Several hundred said they'd arrived at Omarska that morning all from another detention camp, released to this refugee centre after days, sometimes months of interrogation.

We ourselves saw no evidence of beatings on any refugee here, we only heard their allegations, allegations even the camp doctor seemed unable to substantiate in front of our Serb hosts. No one we spoke to knew why they had been brought here, whether they were prisoners or refugees or what lay in store for them. In this civil war there is no sense and a great deal of horrifying cruelty.

Penny Marshall, *News at Ten*, Northern Bosnia.

1993

RUSSIA'S PRESIDENT YELTSIN had to turn to the army in October as left-wing MPs tried to throw him out of power. The MPs had barricaded themselves inside the parliament building – which became known as the Russian White House after a week of protests and riots on the streets of Moscow. Among those inside, leading the rebellion, were Yeltsin's vice-president, and the speaker of the parliament. Yeltsin took one of many big gambles in his career and – unknown to those inside – called in the army. The White House was well defended so when the army's special forces – dressed in black – started arriving a fierce battle was about to begin.

Cameraman Eugene Campbell had had a call from a contact at 2.00am warning that something big might happen. So he and reporter Ian Glover-James were on the streets before dawn. They were in time to

President Yeltsin ordered in Russian tanks to dislodge pro-parliamentary forces from the Russian 'White House' – the parliament building.

see the first column of armoured personnel carriers drive down one of the city's main streets, the Arbat, and then open up with their guns on the White

Impressionist Rory Bremner took his version of Trevor McDonald to new heights with an imaginary 'And Finally' tour.

House. Over the next twenty minutes as it grew lighter, more and more special forces arrived. The problem for Ian and Eugene was that although they were getting good pictures, it was difficult to tell the rest of the ITN team that the fierce battle was breaking out. Ian had to clamber on his hands and knees for twenty minutes to a phone to alert the ITN bureau. Soon Moscow correspondent Julian Manyon and another cameraman, Jon Steele, were on their way to join them.

Eugene remembers crouching behind a two-foot wall as bullets pinged against a plate glass window just above him. He waved a camera cloth – used to wipe the lens – as a white flag. The special forces went into the building with so many guns firing that you couldn't hear an individual shot. The noise had been so deafening that even when it was all over and Eugene went back to his hotel, every time there was a noise, like the sound of a cash register, it sounded like a gunshot.

Julian Manyon and Jon Steele were caught up in another war zone that year where Jon's battlefield training came in very useful. They were reporting the civil war in the former Soviet republic of Georgia. There was heavy fighting around the town of Sukhumi where Georgian government troops were trying to hold the line against the rebels from the Abkahzia region who had laid siege to the city.

The government forces were suffering heavy losses. During the fighting, Jon handed the camera to Julian so he could help a wounded soldier who was bleeding to death. Jon was able to bandage his wounds. Jon went on win cameraman of the year for the pictures he took during that battle and his work in Moscow.

ITN camerman Jon Steele filming the fighting in Georgia between government forces and rebels in Sukhumi, Georgia (top). Jon then helped a wounded soldier who was bleeding to death.

The power of *News at Ten*'s pictures is one of its hallmarks. Yet one programme in July kept the nation riveted by showing the same shot for thirteen minutes and it wasn't even a particularly interesting one. The subject too was rather dry.

The picture in question was a live shot from inside the House of Commons, where the debate was on the European Social Chapter of the Maastricht Treaty. *News at Ten* had been told the vote would be shortly after ten o'clock, but it didn't quite work out like that.

There were behind-the-scenes delays but *News at Ten* didn't want to cut away and miss the vote. In the end, the vote took thirteen minutes longer than anyone expected. Political correspondent Peter Murphy somehow managed to keep talking – without any kind of script – for all that time. But it was an exciting moment. John Major's government lost by one vote. A vote of confidence followed the next day. The minute-by-minute viewing figures showed that hardly any viewers switched away from the programme.

And Finally...

When Pippy the budgie escaped from the house, his owner, Arthur Bendon, feared he would never see his pet again. But Arthur had taken a unique precaution in case this ever happened.

Pippy took refuge in a tree in a nearby street where he was rescued by Ruth Derbin, who took him inside and warmed the little bird with a hairdryer.

As soon as Pippy felt a little more chirpy he started to talk, reciting the address of his own house at Strawberry Close, Nailsea.

Ruth put a note through Arthur's letterbox and he immediately telephoned her. Ruth knew straightaway that Pippy was Arthur's bird. Not only could he tell her where he lived, but Pippy's voice sounded enough like Arthur's for her to recognize him.

The Battle for the Russian White House, 4 October 1993

It was at around seven o'clock this morning that Boris Yeltsin took the fateful step of ordering his troops and tanks to attack the White House and flush out the defenders. Hearing the tanks coming, the parliamentary militia ran to take up their defensive positions. Almost at once the armed vehicles came under fire. As helicopter gun ships circled the White House tower, assault troops moved forward under the cover of the armed car.

They were paratroopers and special forces troops, ready to obey Boris Yeltsin's orders to open fire on Russia's rebel MPs and their defendants.

The order to move in and open fire was apparently given after last-minute talks between the government and the opposition broke down with anger on both sides. The result was the President's decision to save his government, if necessary by bloodshed, and the destruction of parliament. And the building soon began to burn.

The assault soon became a costly affair. Yards from ITN's camera, some of Yeltsin's soldiers were pinned down with a badly wounded comrade who they finally carried off to safety. Civilian volunteers carried the wounded back but for some no amount of medical help could be enough.

At the White House the continuous fire of Yeltsin's forces riddled the front and side of the building and inside the fire spread. The heart of the parliament building was now ablaze. In the open with no cover a man crawled to try and save a wounded soldier. Under fire he dragged his comrade back to shelter although the man's wounds may have been beyond tending.

But the battle had now turned decidedly against the defenders who were forced into the upper floors of the White House tower, when Yeltsin's special forces broke into the floors below.

At about 2.30pm, men with white flags came out of the building, apparently to negotiate. But then dozens more people climbed out of the wreckage to surrender, among them a squad of policemen who had gone over to the opposition only the day before. Those who surrendered included rebel MPs, parliamentary staff and the militia who had tried and failed to defend them.

Shooting is still going on in the area of the White House as troops try to flush out pockets of snipers. It's still not known how many people died in today's battles. An early official figure of 500 dead inside parliament is said to be exaggerated. The White House itself is still ablaze and tonight Boris Yeltsin is the unquestioned master of a smashed and burning parliament.

Julian Manyon, *News at Ten*, Moscow.

1994

GLOBAL WARMING has been much reported on *News at Ten.* It certainly seemed something strange was happening to the weather at the start of the year when floods engulfed parts of southern England. Chichester was one of the worst affected places and South of England reporter Robert Hall regularly did live reports from the waterlogged city.

One particular night *News at Ten* editors said they wouldn't be requiring a 'live-spot' from Robert. In some ways that was welcome news for the camera crew and satellite engineers. They had already spent hours in the cold and pouring rain, with the water rising ever nearer to the two tonnes of satellite equipment – and the 200 volts running through it. They did do a live report for the early evening news, in a blizzard. They were just packing up when a call came through. *News at Ten* editors liked the version of the live report Robert had just done. Could they do it again for *News at Ten*? So they sandbagged the satellite equipment to protect it from the rising water and prepared to see out another fourteen-hour day up to their knees in water. At 9.50pm, the pictures they were beaming back could be seen back at ITN. It was only then that the programme editor decided the scene didn't look quite as good as it had on the early evening news and decided not to run it after all.

Man-made – rather than natural – disasters were never far from our screens. The brutal fighting between the Hutus and the Tutsis in Rwanda

In Rwanda evidence emerged of the massacre of one hundred thousand Tutsis by Hutu fighters.

brought us shocking images during the summer. This was Africa's killing fields. The civil war was both political and tribal. The Hutus ran the government; the Tutsis were the rebels. Their tribal rivalry went back generations.

The true picture of the scale of the killings became clearer when thousands of refugees fleeing the fighting poured across the border into Zaire. Reporter Julian Manyon and a crew were sent to Bukavu on Zaire's border with Rwanda – one of the main crossing points for the refugees. They landed on a grassy airstrip without visas or a satellite phone but ready to tell a story of terrible human suffering. Logistics however conspired against them, not once but several times. After handing over money to a

News at Ten's court artist: Priscilla Coleman

In some courts in the United States cameras are allowed to film the proceedings – who can forget the moment O.J. Simpson was found not guilty of murdering his wife and a male friend of hers, or the moment British au pair Louise Woodward was found guilty of the killing of the baby who was in her care?

In Britain cameras aren't usually allowed into the courts so *News at Ten* uses an artist to sketch the main participants and any dramatic moments there may be, like defendants or witnesses breaking down in tears.

The court artist is Priscilla Coleman. A court rule – Section 41 of the Criminal Justice Act of 1925 – says she isn't allowed to start her sketches inside the court itself, though she is of course allowed to make written notes to help her – as any other journalist would be. She uses crayons, and each drawing takes anything between fifteen minutes to an hour – quick work when you consider each face is an individual portrait and often there can be several faces in one drawing.

She may have to work even faster than that. 'Sometimes you have only the briefest flash of the person you are drawing,' says Priscilla. 'You have to absorb everything. You have to look first at the shape of the face and all the unusual things about it. I kick myself if I miss an important detail like an earring or a mole. As the trial continues the sketches gradually become more realistic as I get more used to the subject.'

When she's finished, her drawings are filmed by the cameraman working on the story, and they can then be edited into the reporter's item to illustrate what went on – or who said what. Among the many famous and infamous faces she has drawn in court are Jeffrey Archer in his libel case, Lester Piggott, Ken Dodd, George Michael, Ernest Saunders, Gillian Taylforth from *EastEnders* and Rosemary West. Perhaps her most embarrassing moment came when she was studying the face of footballer Dean Saunders in court before starting on a drawing of him. His wife got rather angry at Priscilla's interest in him and complained to her solicitor.

Priscilla started her career at college in America, where she studied fine art and graphics. After a stint working for an American television station she moved to Britain with her husband and offered her services to ITN.

There are often calls to the *News at Ten* desk about Priscilla's work after a major trial. Usually they are from barristers' offices asking how they can get a copy of a drawing of a particular lawyer to hang on their walls.

Who is the person she's enjoyed drawing most? Liz Hurley, when she gave evidence against a gang of girls who'd mugged her. 'She is a beautiful woman,' says Priscilla, 'and wonderful to draw.'

Robert Moore reporting on the suffering of the refugees who had escaped from the fighting in Rwanda.

customs post in a grass hut and collecting a receipt which said 'Bribe to enter the country with technical equipment – $200', they set off for the main town. They found a hotel on the edge of Lake Bukavu and while Julian and his cameraman went off to film, producer Angela Frier set about trying to find a satellite phone to ring *News at Ten*. Eventually, with the help of a local driver, Angela found one and called ITN. It was mid morning British time. Already *News at Ten* was desperate for a report from Julian but there was no satellite dish to transmit it from. The nearest town with a dish was Goma, which was several hundred miles away but flights were not reliable. The roads over the mountains were said to

be impassable in places because of mudslides and dangerous after dark because of bandits. Angela said to the foreign desk back at ITN, 'Yes I know it's only half an inch on the map but it's a ten-hour drive.' *News at Ten* wanted a report regardless even though there was only twelve hours to get the report to Goma and editing the report hadn't even started.

Two hours later the edit was finished. Angela and her driver, Simba, set off for the airport to try their luck. There was a flight to Goma scheduled for four o'clock in the afternoon. It never came. Simba suggested she talked to a man who had a plane she might be able to charter. At the far end of the runway was a very smart single-engine Cessna with a man polishing the propeller. Angela remembers the conversation. 'Oh yes, he could take me, no problem. Five hundred dollars? No problem, I said. And as it was getting late I would have to pay to have the landing lights on at Goma. Again, no problem, I told him.' However, it turned out he wasn't insured to fly after dark and he valued his licence.

Angela and Simba then set off to a military airstrip run by the French Foreign Legion. Angela tracked down the colonel in charge, and tape in hand, explained her predicament. He had no planes available but thought there might be a helicopter taking an injured Rwandan general from Kigali to Goma for treatment at the French field hospital. He went into the wireless room to tell his operator to divert the helicopter to Bukavu, to pick up Angela. It wasn't to be. Five minutes later the radio operator came out and said, *'Madame, je suis désolé. Le blessé est mort.'* ('Madam, I'm sorry. The injured man has died.') There would be no helicopter.

So how could Angela tell *News at Ten*? Even the helpful French colonel drew the line at using his satellite phone for a civilian call. To the rescue came a charming French pilot who had just flown in with supplies. He let Angela use his radio and, with her American Express card, she opened an account with Stockholm radio and got through to *News at Ten*, dreading the response. 'Oh don't worry,' came the reply. 'We've changed our minds. In fact we want you to go to Goma to do a *News at Ten* report for tomorrow night.'

Angela went back to the French colonel and arranged to be on one of his cargo flights at 6.00am the following morning. She, Julian and the rest of the crew arrived at quarter to six only to see a cargo plane taxiing down the runway ready for take off. The colonel was shaving. He saw Angela walk behind him in his mirror and turned round and said, *'Merde. J'ai oublié.'* Charitably translated that means, 'Oh dear, I forgot.' Not wanting to lose face, though half of it was covered in shaving foam, he ran outside, told Angela to follow and together they jumped into his open-topped Land Rover. He drove down the middle of the runway waving his arms around like a lunatic. They got round behind the plane which was revving up on its starting blocks. The ramp at the back came down. By this time the rest of the crew had shown up in the other car. Eventually, after much complaining and shouting, the ITN gear was loaded into the plane and off it went. Julian Manyon's *News at Ten* report that night won a Royal Television Society award.

ITN newscaster Dermot Murnaghan suddenly found himself in the middle of a different kind of action when he was filming beside Lake Geneva in Switzerland: a

The damage wreaked on the Chechen capital Grozny by Russian tanks and artillery. Russia was trying to stop the Chechen republic breaking away from its control.

life-saving rescue. He'd seen two children with their nanny playing by the water just as he was about to record his piece to camera. The camera started to roll and Dermot started to deliver his script. He heard a noise and was turning round to ask the children to be quiet when he realized that one of them had disappeared, and the nanny had a look of horror on her face. In the water he saw the face of a little boy about four or five feet under the water looking up at him. Dermot said, 'There was a split second of inertia and a sense of disbelief. You get used to presenting the news but you don't expect to become involved in dramatic incidents.' He then jumped into the water which was about twelve feet deep, still wearing his suit. He managed to rescue the boy and pull him to the edge of the water. Later the boy's parents came over to thank him for saving their son's life – and lent him a dry shirt, a pair of golfing trousers and some trainers, which Dermot had to wear on the plane home.

There was more public-unravelling of the much-troubled marriage of the Prince and Princess of Wales in the summer and something of a scoop for *News at Ten*. The Prince had agreed to do a television interview with Jonathan Dimbleby for an ITV programme marking the twenty-fifth anniversary of the Prince's investiture. Three days before the programme was broadcast ITN's royal correspondent Nicholas Owen got a call from a contact – even now he won't say who from. Nicholas was told the Prince had admitted, during the interview, being unfaithful to Princess Diana. A similar admission from the Princess was to come later in a *Panorama* interview. It was a major story but Nicholas couldn't get confirmation from anyone at Central Television which made the programme nor from Buckingham Palace. For those three days, *News at Ten* was quoted, whenever the story was reported elsewhere. It was an agonizing wait to find out whether the normally reliable contact had been right. One concern was that amid the pressure, the programme-makers could have considered removing that answer. Of course they didn't. Nicholas's contact was vindicated. More importantly perhaps, so was Nicholas.

News at Ten's lead in the TV ratings over its BBC rival reached its highest level for ten years at the start of the summer. In the first six months of the year 6.7 million people were tuned in to Trevor. The number of people watching the *Nine O'Clock News* was 5.8 million.

There was also something to smile about when *News at Ten* produced a video of 'And Finally' stories – introduced by Trevor.

And Finally...

The Victoria Falls are acknowledged as one of the seven natural wonders of the world, but it is very doubtful if Dr Livingstone ever thought his most famous discovery would ever become the mecca of bungee jumpers from around the world.

Jumping from the bridge spanning the gorge, at 111 metres, it was thought to be the highest natural bungee jump in the world.

Described by fans of this sport as the ultimate thrill, experts even go as far as taking a quick dip in the Zambezi before springing back into the air.

However, the price for such a thrill was also rather frightening: £60 a jump.

1995

MANCHESTER UNITED'S Eric Cantona used his feet in the wrong kind of way in January and found himself on the front pages of the newspapers rather than just on the sports pages. He'd kicked a Crystal Palace fan who'd taunted him as he was leaving the field after being sent off. When *News at Ten* sent reporter Terry Lloyd to the Caribbean holiday island of Guadeloupe – where the soccer star was staying – Cantona carried out a similar kind of attack on Terry.

Terry and cameraman Mike Inglis had tried to talk to Cantona inside the private grounds of his hotel but the Frenchman had refused their request for an interview and called the hotel's security. The next day they saw Cantona with his wife and son on a public beach and

President Clinton and his wife Hillary going to dinner with John and Norma Major at Downing Street during a three-day visit to Britain.

A powerful earthquake hit Japan devastating the city of Kobe. Rescue teams trying to find survivors under the rubble.

began to film them. The next thing Terry knew, Cantona had grabbed him in a headlock and said, 'Come with me, I want a chat with you.' He spoke in perfect English, not French as he usually did in news conferences. He tried to drag Terry into the hotel's private grounds. Then he let Terry go and turned his attention to Mike and tried to lead him away. Suddenly Cantona ran at Terry and kicked him with both feet – kung fu style. Terry said, 'It was like an action replay of his attack on the Crystal Palace fan. I knew just how that man must have felt. I fell into the sand and he punched me. He nearly cracked my ribs. It is incredible that a man facing prosecution should go and do the same thing again.' Terry's ribs were badly bruised in the attack. And his regard for the player was damaged too.

Andrew Simmons reporting from the Chechen capital Grozny on the continuing assault by Russian forces on the breakaway region.

You often read about people getting exorbitant phone bills and then it turns out that it's the phone company that has got its sums wrong. The same thing happened to ITN in April when a bill arrived from British Telecom for £42,000. Admittedly, ITN's BT bill includes the price of satellite bookings which can cost hundreds of pounds. Had the bill been correct, *News at Ten*'s coverage of foreign news could have been curtailed. The foreign stories at the time were the Oklahoma bombing, the French presidential elections and a massacre in Rwanda. As it turned out the bill had been paid . What's more, in double-checking the figures, the the accounts department found that in fact BT owed ITN £21,000.

The battle for control of the Chechen capital, Grozny, marked perhaps the bloodiest phase in the former Soviet republic's civil war. The Chechens wanted to break away from Russian control. President Yeltsin sent in his army to stop them. The Chechens were good guerrilla fighters and many said the Russian army didn't really have the stomach for that kind of war. Julian Manyon was the reporter sent to cover the fighting. Without doubt, it was a dangerous place in which to work.

Julian says, 'I don't go to Chechnya because I like it. Few correspondents do. There's little of the glamour and none of the comforts of reporting some past wars. But it's a "David and Goliath" story that simply has to be told.' The name Grozny means 'terrible' and Julian remembers a twinge of fear as he returned to the city. No wonder. It was a war of snipers and helicopter gunships that appeared from nowhere. A war in which the Russian army used its massive firepower without seeming to care a great deal about where the shells fell.

Julian came across a group of rebels, whose commanders told him were preparing to attack a Russian strong-point on the main road outside Grozny. The battle for that strong-point began the following day and Julian and his cameraman Simon Llewellyn got caught up in it. They approached the Russian position on foot, displaying both a white flag and Union Jack. A Russian soldier behind the sandbags shouted to Julian to get out as they were expecting a fight to start. Julian did a quick piece to camera and got it right in one take. As Julian says, 'Adrenaline is a wonderful thing.' Then he and Simon ran for the car. As they did so a Russian television cameraman came the other way and they shouted at him to come

John Major announced that he wanted an election for the leadership of the Conservative party. It was a challenge to his back-bench critics but they failed to unseat him.

Julia Somerville

Julia Somerville joined ITN in 1987 from the BBC where she had been a senior presenter of the *Nine O'Clock News*. During her time at ITN she has presented all the main weekday and weekend programmes. She was one of the regular team of newscasters on *News at Ten* until the programme's major change in 1992 when Trevor McDonald became the sole presenter. She is now the co-presenter of ITN's *Lunchtime News* and also occasionally presents *News at Ten*. She fronted *3D* – a current affairs series on ITV.

Julia's journalistic career started after graduating from Sussex University. She joined IPC Magazines working on *Homes and Gardens* and *Woman's Journal* and then joined the PR section of *Woman's Own*. She spent two years as editor of a computer group's house magazine before joining the BBC in 1973 as a sub-editor in the Radio Newsroom. She became a chief-sub editor and then a reporter and was made labour affairs correspondent in 1981. She joined the BBC's *Nine O'Clock News* in 1984.

Julia is patron of the British Brain and Spine Foundation.

The former trader with Barings Bank, Nick Leeson, arriving in Singapore to face trial over his part in the collapse of the bank.

with them. But he kept on walking. Minutes later the firing started. Julian and Simon were driving at speed away from the Russian position when two bullets whistled past the car. The Russian cameraman, they learned later, was shot dead on the spot.

The attack on the Russian strong-point made a powerful television package. But Julian says he couldn't help thinking about the Russian cameraman. He was the nineteenth journalist to die in twenty months of war. 'To work as a war correspondent in Grozny,' says Julian, 'you need some judgement and also, a lot of luck.'

The Queen met South Africa's President, Nelson Mandela, for the first time on a visit to Durban. It was to be the grand finale of the royal tour. The Queen and the President were to appear together on the balcony of Durban's town hall. Reporter Mark Austin

and his crew were in the crowds waiting for Mr Mandela to arrive. They were the only ITN crew – the BBC had three. Mark's crew got good pictures of Mr Mandela doing a walk-about. Meanwhile one of the BBC crews and their reporter had gone to the door of the town hall to interview Mr Mandela. As the President went up the steps of the town hall, to the balcony, he gave the BBC their interview. Mark's crew were stuck outside the security cordon. When Mr Mandela reached the balcony, he saw Mark in the crowd and called out, 'Mark Austin, from ITN, please come and join me up here.' Mark got the interview and amazing pictures of Mr Mandela in front of the crowds below.

And Finally...

The human mind is capable of many amazing feats. To demonstrate mind over matter a team of motivators convinced a number of people that they could walk over hot coals in bare feet. Taking four hours to prepare, the candidates walked the fiery path without any apparent ill effects.

1996

MANY JOURNALISTS are hardened to some of the worst things that go on in the world – because all too often the shocking or the unpalatable are what makes news. The massacre of young children in Dunblane in central Scotland was one of those stories that disturbed everyone, not just those out covering the story but the production teams in the newsroom too. The first reports that flashed up on the *News at Ten* computer screens initially gave no clue of just how many children had been killed. Through the morning the total rose to what seemed an unbelievable number. In the end sixteen children and one of their teachers died.

Colin Baker was one of the reporters sent to cover the story. He has been in some of the worst trouble spots in the world and spent ten years in Belfast but still finds Dunblane hard to talk about. He says it was the worst story he had ever covered, even though there was no personal threat to him. He has never looked back at what his crew filmed that day – those haunting pictures, shot from a distance, of parents running to the school to find out if their children were among those who died. Colin remembers the stewardesses on the British Midland flight up there packing them a bag of sandwiches because they realized Colin's day was going to be a long one. When his *News at Ten* report was finally done, Colin remembers going into a deserted curry house in a heartbroken town. And he remembers the next morning being out filming at dawn watching the

Dunblane primary school where Thomas Hamilton shot dead sixteen children and their teacher (top). Flowers and toys lined the streets of Dunblane in memory of the young victims of the massacre (above). ITn reporter Colin Baker remembers the massacre as the worst story he has covered in his career.

Trevor McDonald, OBE

Trevor McDonald began his television career in his native Trinidad in 1962, where he read the nightly news and was later an interviewer on local current affairs programmes. Prior to that he had worked for newspapers and in local radio. He joined the BBC World Service in 1969.

Trevor joined ITN as a reporter in 1973; some of his main assignments were in Northern Ireland. In 1978 he became sports correspondent. He was appointed diplomatic correspondent in 1980, and two years later he took the same title at *Channel 4 News*; he was promoted to diplomatic editor in 1987.

During 1989 he presented ITN's *News at 5.40*, *Channel 4 News* and ITN's weekend programmes.

He had been part of *News at Ten*'s regular presenting team since the beginning of 1990, and became sole anchorman when the programme underwent its major revamp in 1992.

He was awarded the OBE in the New Year's Honours Lists in 1992.

In the last five years Trevor has won numerous awards recognizing him as Britain's top newscaster. He also holds eight honorary doctorates.

He has written biographies of West Indian players Viv Richards and Clive Lloyd, while his autobiography was published in 1993. Trevor's love of poetry resulted in a regular poetry column in the *Daily Telegraph* and the publication of an anthology entitled *Favourite Poems* in October 1997.

milkman and the postman start work as Dunblane woke up to a world that was now without some of its brightest stars.

ITN's coverage of the story was always respectful and went on to win several awards, but the people of Dunblane had more reason than most not to want the media overrunning their town. Yet, says Colin, when he went into the town's supermarket everyone was both polite and totally without animosity.

The people of Chechnya were enjoying a ceasefire after some bloody battles the year before between Chechens fighting for independence and the Russian forces trying to stop them. Reporter Andrew Simmons was assigned to file a special report for *News at Ten* from Grozny in March on the destruction to the capital and on the work of a British charity called 'Merlin'. By now Russia had got military control of the breakaway republic if not quite political control.

Andrew, cameraman Brian McVeigh and producer Oleg Yuriev headed into the capital from their base in Vladikavkaz on what they thought was going to be a straightforward assignment: to film the destruction wreaked on the city. On day one, they'd filmed a shelter for the sick and those too old and frail to escape the city. They lived in dreadful conditions with little food or medicine. The nurse who ran the place dug graves every other day in what used to be the home's gardens to bury those who died. The ITN team had returned to the home for a few extra shots on the second day of filming. They were now on the furthest side of the city in terms of getting back to Vladikavkaz. Oleg said he knew a different route out of the city that would get them back quicker and before it got too dark. What happened next was the kind of thing ITN crews hope will happen only in battlefield training courses.

All had been well until at one checkpoint a Russian soldier said calmly in English: 'Some shooting ahead

Kevin and Ian Maxwell were acquitted of fraud after an eight-month trial. They were found not guilty over the millions missing from the Mirror Group pension fund.

– be careful.' It was the kind of warning reporters often hear in war zones; but there is never room for complacency. Andrew and Brian were in the back of the car. They both had the feeling that something was wrong. There were no other cars on the road until, that is, they turned a corner and there was a yellow Lada in the middle of the road. Two Russian soldiers were staggering around it. One had an AK-47 rifle in one hand and a plastic bottle of vodka in the other. A few shots rang out like the backfire from a car. The Lada drove off at speed and the ITN car was now a few feet from the Russians.

Before Andrew could take in what was happening, the front passenger door was opened and Oleg was being pulled out. Oleg, a calm, trusted veteran of all things Russian, was trying to reason with an obviously drunken young captain who, in between shouts, was swigging from his plastic bottle which was half full of vodka. His fellow soldier, smelling of vodka but not as drunk, started to search the front of the car. The driver of their special bullet-proof car, Egor, was terrified and appeared to be frozen. He could understand the words of the soldier jostling Oleg outside. As Andrew said later, 'Brian and I were in not-so-blissful ignorance of what was being said. In hindsight it was one of those

In the continuing fighting in Chechnya a group of hostages were kidnapped from a hospital by Chechen rebels (top). A Chechen rebel crouching beside the bus that contained the hostages in a military standoff with the Russian army (above).

rare moments on foreign assignments when you were better off without a simultaneous translation.' Only much later was Oleg able to recount what they were saying: 'We are going to kill you all.'

As the soldiers rummaged through the glove compartment of the ITN car, Andrew muttered to Brian 'This doesn't look good. Whatever happens, we mustn't move from here. We have to play for time.' Andrew remembers the words exactly. 'Both Brian and I knew that with Oleg out of the car there could be no "Starsky and Hutch" escapes with screeching

tyres. We feared the worst for Oleg but we were powerless to do anything but stall. The soldier inside the car started jabbering at me. I acted the British idiot and started fumbling for passes and saying in the minuscule Russian I knew, "English journalist".'

The other soldier pointed his gun at the rear passenger window of the car, right behind Andrew's head, and made several gestures. It was obvious he wanted Andrew to get out. Andrew carried on pretending not to understand until the soldier lowered his gun and fired three single shots. Apart from the ringing in Andrew's ears, he could hear the right rear tyre going down. Oleg then started again with his attempt at cool persuasion. It didn't work.

'The drunken soldiers could easily have dragged me out,' says Andrew, 'but for some reason they didn't.' The second soldier got back inside the car and started rummaging around on the floor. He started shouting and then pointed his gun at the passengers. Oleg nodded to Andrew to indicate the time had come for him to get out of the car. Oleg once again tried another approach but the soldier hit him on the side of the head with the butt of his rifle. Oleg fell to the ground. The drunken soldier kicked him repeatedly on his head and body. Andrew pointed to Oleg and shouted to the other soldier, 'What's going on?'

Andrew remembers that terrifying moment clearly. 'There was no answer, just a grasp of my arm and walk to a ditch at the side of the road. It was such a hopeless position to be in. I find it hard to describe my thoughts at the time. My mind was fixed on Oleg. He was badly beaten and the soldier was dragging him towards our line-up. He appeared semi-conscious and his attacker was now fiddling with his AK-47. I thought, "Oh God, he's going to shoot him dead in front of us." For some reason, I brought out a packet of cigarettes and offered one to the soldier who was standing in front of me, Brian and Egor. Perhaps I was just trying to buy time. The soldier looked utterly bemused and shook his head. I then turned to the "animal" standing over Oleg and this, I remember, was a dangerous moment. It was my first eye contact with the soldier. I had deliberately avoided it up to now. I offered my packet to him. It seemed obvious what he wanted to do. I think he was working up to the sort of frenzy in which he could pull the trigger. Perhaps what threw him was the ridiculous act of a Marlboro being offered. There was a pause, then a grimace, followed by a conversation between the two soldiers.'

What happened next was extraordinary – the timing, incredible. There was a shout from somewhere down the road in the direction the Lada had driven. The soldiers then started shouting too. Soon the voice became the figure of a burly Russian officer who promptly started arguing with the two officers.

Andrew, Brian and Egor saw their chance. They grabbed Oleg, bundled him into the car and jumped in after him. They clicked the central locking and Egor drove off, on three tyres. The less-drunken soldier jumped on to the bonnet of the car, smashing the windscreen with the butt of his AK-47, before falling off. The other fired at the rear passenger window. There was a crack like the sound of a stone hitting a windscreen. Later, when they stopped to give Oleg some first aid, Andrew could see what had happened. 'There was a strike mark on the rear passenger window. Had the glass not been bullet proof it would have killed me and probably Egor as well.' When Oleg got to hospital his injury was diagnosed as a hairline fracture of the skull. As Andrew says, 'He is a brave man who kept his cool and undoubtedly helped save our lives.'

News at Ten lost one of its most famous names in May. She wasn't a newscaster but had been a member of the *News at Ten* family for twenty-two years. When the death of reporter Joan Thirkettle was announced there were tears in the newsroom that morning. Only a handful of people at ITN had known she'd got cancer. To everyone else it came as a terrible

The IRA ceasefire ended with the Docklands bombing. Two men were killed. The Home Secretary Michael Howard toured the scene of the bombing.

shock. She was forty-eight but always seemed younger and was still at the top of her powers and her profession. That was what made her death shocking. She was modest in a business where many are not. 'I'm not important at all,' she once said. 'The story is what is important and the pictures that tell it.' She treated the most junior producer as if they were the most important journalist in the newsroom. She perfected the technique that all television journalists strive for, of turning a complicated story into a straightforward one. Joan was a general reporter who had her specialities without being a specialist reporter and she could get to grips with any story in a short time. She had many highlights in her career at ITN – one perhaps was on the day of the death of the Labour leader John Smith. He was rushed to Bart's hospital from where Joan reported live throughout the morning in a two-hour special programme that was to win a prestigious award from the Royal Television Society.

As an interviewer she had the tact, patience and charm to win the confidence of people who for whatever reason did not normally like to be interviewed. These qualities could be seen in two very different examples. The first involved Salman

News at Ten reporter Joan Thirkettle (above) who died in May; with Salman Rushdie (below).

interview. Joan told her newsdesk that the author would turn up at ITN to talk to her. Some didn't quite believe her. Then, sure enough, surrounded by security men, he appeared and spoke to Joan.

The second involved a boy called Stephen Wilshire. He was autistic but had a hidden talent. She persuaded ITN to take him to New York where, from memory, he produced sketches of the Manhattan skyline in astonishing detail.

And Finally...

Local parishioners decided that their church, St John the Divine, in Kennington, South London, needed a little ... something. So they decided to add gargoyles to the spire.

But not the traditional leering gargoyles. They wanted something different for their church.

Now the spire is adorned with gargoyle caricatures of local teachers, pensioners and clergy.

As the church stands on land owned by the Duchy of Cornwall, Prince Charles's face is there, along with carvings of Queen Elizabeth and the Queen Mother. The Queen was said to have been delighted with the idea and readily gave permission for the carvings to be made.

Rushdie. When he first learned the implications of the Iranian death threat against him and went into hiding, there was great competition among some of the biggest names in journalism to get that first

1997

ONE OF THE MOST important and colourful stories of the year was the handover of Hong Kong to China. Hong Kong had belonged to Britain under a long lease that was due to run out at midnight on 30 June. For weeks, *News at Ten* had been covering the build up – with reports on troops and ex-pats gradually and tearfully saying goodbye and others on how Hong Kong might fare under its new Chinese leaders.

Because it was such a big, colourful, story *News at Ten* was to be presented from Hong Kong by Trevor McDonald on the night of the handover. A production team flew out with him ahead of the big day to prepare. It was going to be a long day. It was certainly a wet one. The last Governor of Hong Kong, Chris Patten, stood in the rain outside Government House as the Union Jack was lowered for the last time that morning. It was an emotional moment, like many others that day. No one was sure whether it was rain or a tear that ran down Mr Patten's face.

The handover – at midnight – took place at 6.00pm British time – just at the end of ITN's early evening news. Trevor did a live report and the team was able to send pictures of the Royal Yacht *Britannia* pulling away from Hong Kong harbour with Prince Charles and Chris Patten on board just before the end of that programme. Then everyone had to gear up again for *News at Ten* – which would be at dawn Hong Kong time. Trevor was to broadcast from the top of the Mandarin Hotel. It provided a lovely backdrop of

Mark Austin reporting on the ceremony to mark the handover of Hong Kong from British to Chinese rule.

twinkling lights from the skyscrapers and from around the lagoon.

The makeshift control room where the director, sound engineer and production assistant had to sit was a tiny, airless, windowless storeroom two floors below but linked by cables. It was a hot night, made hotter for those who had to run up and down the stairs – the lifts didn't go that far up.

The team had always known from the start that there was a danger that the start of July could coincide with an early monsoon season. And so it proved. With fifteen minutes to go before the start of the programme, Trevor was in position on the roof, sitting on a high stool and rehearsing. In the stifling

Trevor McDonald preparing to present *News at Ten* from Hong Kong on handover night – before the monsoon struck.

control room, communications were established with the studio control room in London. With five minutes to go, a kind of mist descended. Those twinkling lights slowly faded from view. Then it started to rain. The only shelter was a large canvas awning – intended to provide rooftop sunbathers with a little shade, not a TV news anchorman, three cameras, numerous lights and a teleprompt machine with protection against a monsoon.

The awning was being buffeted by the wind. When the heavens opened the rain fell so heavily it didn't run off the awning, it made it bulge with water instead. There was a real danger that it was going to either tear or bring the whole thing crashing down on top of Trevor and the equipment. Trevor valiantly read the introduction to each of the reports by the correspondents with him in Hong Kong. During each report there was just enough time to push the water out of the awning from below using brushes. The wind made things even worse. Two of the team had to hang on to either end of the awning on stepladders, to stop it buckling from the weight of the water and from blowing away in gusts of storm-force winds. All the while, one of the engineers desperately trying to push the water out of the awning kept shouting, 'It's going to go, it's going to go.' No one at home would have noticed a thing, apart perhaps from the sound of the rain on the awning, until one particular gust blew some of the water over Trevor's shoulder towards the end of the programme. They certainly wouldn't have guessed the seriousness of the situation from Trevor's demeanour. He played a blinder. When he said, 'Goodnight from Hong Kong,' the problems weren't over. The crew had to carry the cameras, lights and teleprompt machine back inside yet still keep hold of the awning. Only when everything was safely put away did everyone realize how dangerous the situation had been. Firstly the awning could have come

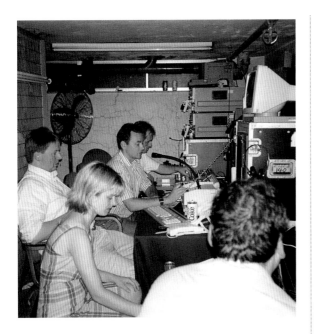

The cramped makeshift control room in Hong Kong's Mandarin hotel.

down. Secondly, with all cameras and lights in inches of water there could have been an electric shock at any moment. Thirdly, those clinging to the awning could have been knocked over the balcony by it and fallen twenty floors to the ground.

What was the biggest story of the year, certainly in the working lives of many of the *News at Ten* team, came in the early hours of the morning on 31 August. The first details of the crash involving Diana, Princess of Wales, and Dodi Fayed in a gloomy Paris underpass proved to be wrong. Early reports said Dodi was dead. That of course was true. One also said Diana had walked away from the accident. That certainly wasn't. Others said Diana was badly injured but alive, which was true for a time.

Newscaster Dermot Murnaghan with colleague and royal correspondent Nicholas Owen were rushed into the ITN building, as were dozens of production teams and journalists. It was the kind of situation ITN regularly rehearses – a disaster, or the death of a senior figure in public life. No one

ever thought it would be Diana in such shocking circumstances. ITN went on the air once everyone was in place and stayed on the air for most the day. At first there was real disbelief. There's something about being woken in the middle of the night that, even for journalists, makes shocking news hard to assimilate. Then came the first pictures of the crumpled Mercedes. It started to seem like the nightmare could be true. Even when news of her death did come through, no one could quite believe it.

Trevor presented a *News at Ten*-style main evening news programme – with his normal production team around him – that Sunday night. Royal correspondent Nicholas Owen remembers the impact of the day. He had been in the studio all day helping to broadcast the facts of what had happened. It wasn't until he went down to Diana's home, Kensington Palace, that the real magnitude of the story began to sink in. The gardens around the palace were by then in darkness. 'They were full of people,' says Nicholas, 'yet it was so silent.' Nicholas has no hesitation in saying it was ITN that captured the mood of the day. 'That is one of ITN's strengths,' he says. 'Strong presentation in the studio allied with a close rapport with the public.'

One of Diana's last public campaigns – against landmines in Angola.

The death of Diana, Princess of Wales. Flowers carpeted the grounds of her home at Kensington Palace (top left). A young admirer remembering the 'People's Princess' (above). The gun carriage carrying the Princess's coffin (top right) and the flowers from her sons with – in boyish writing – a card marked simply 'Mummy' (above right).

During the week between Diana's death and her funeral the following weekend *News at Ten* reported on how the public tried to come to terms with the death of the most famous woman in the world and how the Royal Family grappled with the protocol of commemorating the death of a modern princess – the People's Princess. There were moving and extraordinary scenes as her sons, Princes William and Harry returned from Balmoral to Buckingham Palace to thank people for their sympathy. There was also the extraordinary sight of the Queen broadcasting from Buckingham Palace, to acknowledge the public's sadness and pay her own tribute to Diana. ITN was on the air again throughout the day of her funeral, with Trevor anchoring the programme. Once again it was ITN who showed the grief on the faces of people in the crowds in Hyde Park, along the funeral route and around Westminster Abbey, rather than just those inside the Abbey. In the evening Trevor presented another extended news programme rounding off a quite incredible week. Nicholas Owen says on the Diana story, as on many others, ITN allows its correspondents to 'tell it like it is'. He says throughout that week he was given total freedom to report it how he wanted.

As *News at Ten*'s anchorman, Trevor would of course normally present the programme most nights of the week and usually on big set-pieces like the handover

The changing face of graphics

When *News at Ten* first started, most of the programme's graphics, like maps, were made out of cardboard and put in front of a camera. Text was done using Letraset. The camera could zoom in or pull out to give an impression of movement. The only form of animation was by hand. That meant strips of cardboard could be slid into or pulled out of the cardboard graphic to give the appearance of movement.

So for example, *News at Ten*'s own economic indicator of the early 1980s – the Job Survey – would have cardboard strips hiding the placenames of where jobs were being created or lost. When the cardboard strip was pulled out, the name of the town or city would be revealed. By today's standards it was very unsophisticated and very labour intensive too – not only in the Letrasetting but also during transmission when one or more people had to remove the strips of card.

The Job Survey – like the rest of ITN's graphics – eventually became computerized. ITN invented its own computer graphics system called VT80. Graphics could then be prepared electronically and the images created could be sent electronically into the studio – cutting out the need for a camera. Maps were stored on disks and could be amended by computer programmers who could instruct the computer what changes to make.

What's more, VT80 could animate – it could make things appear and disappear. So using the Job Survey example it could add or remove names and places at the push of a button. And it could move things around on the screen. Computer graphics are seen at their best perhaps on General Election nights, but every night on *News at Ten* there is always at least one graphics sequence.

Long before Peter Snow became attached to his swingometers at the BBC, he pioneered a different kind of illustration as ITN's diplomatic correspondent – what was to become known as the 'sand table'. During the Six Day War in the Middle East, just before *News at Ten* began, the only way of giving an overview of what was happening was to make a large model of the area, complete with mountains, rivers and sea. Peter could stand behind the model or 'sand table' and move tanks and ships around to give an impression of what was happening. Now computer graphics have advanced so far that they can be made to show things in three dimensions. *News at Ten* still uses the old 'sand table' idea to give an overview of what is happening in a particular trouble spot – with a reporter standing behind a relief map with planes and boats moving around. Now, though, once the artwork has been painstakingly prepared, it can all be done at the push of a few buttons.

of Hong Kong and the death of Diana. In his absence, colleagues would stand in for him. One of Trevor's holidays coincided with the thirtieth anniversary of *News at Ten*. For Dermot Murnaghan, who was presenting the programme that night, it seemed that life had come full circle. He remembered being interested in news as a boy in Northern Ireland, and badgering his father to let him stay up and watch the first *News at Ten*. Now here he was, presenting the programme himself.

Towards the end the year ITN took delivery of yet another advance in television cameras. The new cameras recorded their pictures digitally on to tape. The tapes and therefore the cameras were more compact. More importantly perhaps digital

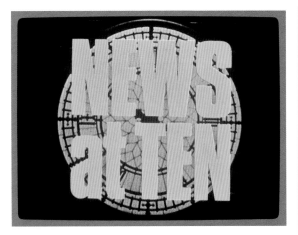

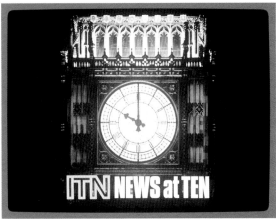

The changing clock faces of *News at Ten* over its thirty-two-year run.

recording using the new DVC-Pro system meant the quality of the image was high and could be copied or edited without any drop in that quality.

The ever-changing technology also brought another advance for filing *News at Ten* reports from more and more inaccessible parts of the world. The ITN satellite dish remained the preferred option but there are still some places where the cargo plane, boat or truck needed to transport the dish can't operate. In the summer ITN bought two encoding devices which can store pictures from a camera tape digitally and then replay them via a satellite telephone back to London. The system is called 'store and forward'. The units are about the size of a briefcase. Reporters in

far-flung locations usually have satellite phones with them anyway. The new ITN system was used for the first time by Paul Davies in Sierra Leone. Because there are so many 'digits' needed to store and then re-create television pictures it can take quite a long time to send them all down a telephone line. It takes just over thirty minutes to transmit one minute of video so Paul's report of one minute forty seconds took nearly an hour to record. Since then it has been used to cover such things as a climbing expedition in the Himalayas by Sir Chris Bonington, and a visit by Prince Charles to Nepal.

Tony Blair's carefully orchestrated general election campaign brought a smile to the face of ITN reporter Mark Webster, who was assigned to cover Mr Blair. Mr Blair's press secretary, Alastair Campbell, came up to Mark and said, 'Tony is speaking at seven this

evening but he wants to do something spontaneous.' Mark asked when. With a little twinkle in his eye, Mr Campbell replied, 'At seven minutes past seven.'

News at Ten's Wales correspondent Tim Rogers found out for himself just what a fiery temper Liam Gallagher, the lead singer in Oasis, has when it comes to dealing with journalists. Tim had been 'doorstepping' – waiting around on a doorstep – on another story in Cardiff to get pictures of Gary Glitter who was appearing in Cardiff at the time of the child pornography case against him. It had been wet and cold and Tim and his cameraman had gone to a nearby hotel to get a warming cup of tea in the foyer.

By chance Liam showed up in the same hotel. Oasis were playing that night in the city's International Arena. Liam had been surrounded by newspaper journalists wanting to know about his latest 'bad-boy' incident at the previous night's concert in Glasgow. Tim went to say hello to some of the reporters and then went back to his seat. Liam was clearly getting irritated by the other reporters' questions and then challenged them to a fight. Bearing in mind the large minders he had with him, the reporters decided to leave him alone. Liam then turned his attention to Tim, and came and sat next to him. Tim said, 'Pleased to meet you,' but that was a trigger for a stream of abuse and swearing. It ended when Liam poured the dregs from some glasses that had been left on the

table over Tim's head. There was something of a happy end to this depressing story. A woman dressed as a Christmas tree (it was December) kindly offered to clean Tim up with a box of tissues.

And Finally...

George Shields had a shed at the bottom of his garden. Like many men, he liked to spend time in it. Unlike many men, if Mr Shields felt like going for a drive he could do that in the shed, too.

When George failed to obtain a pony and trap to take a friend to his wedding, he built the petrol-powered shed and took him in that instead.

With a top speed of fifty-five miles per hour, the shed is officially described as 'an agricultural vehicle'. Mr Shields continued using it to raise money for charity.

1998

THE YEAR STARTED AND ENDED with high drama over President Bill Clinton's affair with White House trainee Monica Lewinsky. The news first broke in January and it was clearly a huge story. The President insisted then that he hadn't had a sexual relationship with Miss Lewinsky. When the President was due to make his State of the Union address, presenting *News at Ten* from Washington looked like a good idea. Trevor McDonald and a production team were flown out.

It seemed hard to believe there could be a bigger story on that otherwise quiet Sunday night but within an hour of the *News at Ten* team arriving in ITN's Washington bureau there was one. The computer screens in Washington, and of course in London, reported that the Queen Mother had had a fall. It wasn't clear at that stage how poorly she was but any accident involving a ninety-seven-year-old lady might turn out to be serious. Her Majesty needed an emergency hip operation and of course recovered. In the early hours of the morning in Washington no one could be sure that was how it would turn out. There were lengthy transatlantic phone calls and the decision was taken to fly the *News at Ten* team back. Happily by the time Trevor returned to London the Queen Mother seemed to be out of any danger. The same could not be said of Bill Clinton's presidency.

In April and May *News at Ten* did more than any other news programme anywhere in the world to

The pitiful figure of a child supported by an aid worker (top) and people waiting at a feeding centre in Sudan (above).

highlight the suffering of the people of Southern Sudan as they struggled against the double killers of drought and civil war. ITN's Africa correspondent Tim Ewart was the reporter assigned to the story.

Trevor McDonald and the *News at Ten* production team in the newsroom.

Tim says what sets Sudan apart from other countries facing starvation is that it has no real overland access. There are no suitable roads. Food sent by river or train regularly got hijacked. The whole operation had to be carried out by air. Food had to be flown into the feeding centres, as well as dropped to more remote areas. There was also the sheer distances involved – Sudan is almost the size of Europe.

Tim was the first to report from the town of Wau, which is a four-hour flight from Khartoum, with government permission. Tim also flew into the rebel-held areas on a flight from Kenya. Again, because of the difficulties of travelling, Tim and his crew had to camp out overnight but that is no hardship compared to the suffering of the people whose stories they had come to tell. What was difficult was working in such heat – forty-five degrees centigrade in the shade – and carrying equipment. The team were drinking six litres of water a day each and needing every drop. Tim says,

Panacier, Southern Sudan, 13 May 1998

Sunrise at Panacier. Already it is hot. They wake their children and douse their fires, the daily ritual of survival is about to begin.

The queue outside Panacier is longer than yesterday; the orphans come in first then the mothers and their children. The men are kept outside - they forage where they can. But it is all very orderly: patience is a virtue of the starving.

They sing: `We are bones, we are skin, hunger has taken us.' Would you sing if you were starving? But then that's Africa's way - sing and someone might help. But help here is in short supply. Panacier has not had food or medicines for over a fortnight and stocks will run out on Friday. Seven children died here yesterday.

How much more of this must we see to be convinced that something dreadful is happening here? How more awful must the pictures on your screen become? How thin must they be before they give in and fall down?

The old suffer terribly. They are at the end of the line: the least food, the least attention. Some will have already had their last meal. Yet they make no sound, no gestures - they know the rules, they expect nothing.

For the first time in their little lives, these children must pray that the rains will wait, so that they may live. And those of us with return tickets out of here will pray for them in anger. Anger and despair.

Michael Nicholson, *News at Ten*, Panacier, Southern Sudan.

'What we saw is really only the tip of the iceberg. To drive more than an hour from the feeding centres is impossible. The people you see at the feeding centres are the fittest ones – the ones who have been able to walk for four or five days on foot.'

There is, says Tim, a real dilemma. 'Is it right for us to invade the privacy of these people with cameras that are intrusive and totally unfamiliar when they have so little time left to live?' He justifies it in two ways. 'Firstly,' he says, 'mothers and fathers will hold their children up, so the cameras can see them in the hope that they will receive help. Secondly, these sort of pictures, especially on British television, have a very direct impact and led to millions of pounds of aid contributions.' As Tim says, 'It is nice once in a while do to a story that does some good.'

Few people have ever heard Gerry Adams say sorry – but ITN's Ireland correspondent John Irvine received an apology from the Sinn Fein president when John was covering peace talks in Dublin for *News at Ten*. The Northern Ireland peace process had been making big strides forward – culminating in the Good Friday Agreement. But being such a vitally important issue with so many interests at stake, the process was slow and often frustrating – especially for Sinn Fein when they were temporarily excluded because of the IRA's involvement in two murders.

At the end of one very long day, Gerry Adams came out of discussions at Dublin Castle to talk to the media. There were several cameramen present, but few reporters. John asked him a number of questions about Sinn Fein's links with the IRA – all of which Mr Adams adeptly sidestepped. As John kept probing, Mr Adams appeared to lose his temper, and accused the *News at Ten* man of asking 'smart-arsed' questions. Mr Adams was under quite a lot of pressure at the time but it was an uncharacteristic outburst from a politician who is normally cordial and measured when he talks to journalists. Incidentally, Mr Adams's outburst was the lead story

Tired Mo Mowlam, Secretary of State for Northern Ireland, after the Good Friday Agreement.

that night on the Irish Republic's equivalent of *News at Ten*. That night the Irish Department of Foreign Affairs had a dinner at a Dublin restaurant. John was applauded after his run-in with Mr Adams, but it was notoriety not to be relished. A serious fall-out with Mr Adams could have created problems back in Northern Ireland, but fortunately the problem was solved – by Mr Adams himself.

At a press conference two days later and carried live by several networks, Gerry Adams's opening remark was, 'Is Johnny Irvine here?' Tentatively, among the dozens of seated journalists, a hand went up and a voice said, 'Hello.' 'I'm sorry I annoyed you the other day,' said Mr Adams. 'Don't worry about it,' John replied. 'It had been a long day for both of us.'

John faced a far more exacting and distressing assignment in August: the bombing of Omagh. Twenty-nine lives were lost – more than in any other terrorist attack in Northern Ireland. The Good Friday Peace Agreement was supposed to have put an end to the indiscriminate bombings of the previous thirty years. A terrorist group called 'Real IRA' didn't see it that way. The town was full of shoppers and shopworkers when their bomb went off. For John who knew the town well it was especially distressing.

The ceasefire in Northern Ireland was shattered by the bombing of Omagh in County Tyrone. Twenty-nine people died. Police searched for evidence (top) in the town's High Street (above).

On the following evening, the *News at Ten* team produced a special news programme on the bombing, presented by Trevor. There was little ITN teams in Omagh could do other than report the terrible thing that had taken place. However, they did get to hear of a ten-year-old boy who was in a coma as a result of the bomb. He was in hospital in Enniskillen. His mother eventually helped to bring him round by talking about his favourite football team, Leeds United. A call from ITN's sports desk to the club resulted in the boy receiving a hospital visit from George Graham, the team's manager at the time.

Football fever gripped the country – north and south of the border – during the World Cup finals in France. The night Scotland were defeated 3–0 by Morocco, Norway caused a major shock by defeating the favourites, Brazil. Sports correspondent Graham Miller had to edit a very late Scotland report for the top story on *News at Ten*. Once he'd done that he had to stand by to do a live report with questions from Trevor, immediately afterwards.

On the way to the live position, Graham's sports producer with him in Paris received a call from *News at Ten* asking Graham not to mention the Brazil game, as that was going to be reported nearer the end of the programme in the Sports News section. Graham took the request on board and prepared to talk about the future of Scottish football. There then followed a classic case of crossed wires. Trevor's question came as something of a surprise. 'We were all shocked by Brazil's defeat here in Britain, Graham. What's been the reaction to it in France?' Graham had not even seen the game because he'd been concentrating on Scotland. Graham said later. 'What I wanted to say was, "Hang on, Trevor, you don't want to know about Brazil." My answer was worthy of a waffle of the year award!'

Later in the competition, millions of armchair fans were on the edge of their seats for one of the most dramatic matches ever – England *v* Argentina – in which David Beckham was sent off and England lost in a penalty shootout. During the day *News at Ten* had spoken to one very important viewer about whether she would be watching the match. Scotland correspondent Harry Smith caught up with the Queen during a visit to Dundee and asked her if she would be sitting down with millions of others in front of the television. 'I don't know,' replied Her Majesty, 'what time is it on?' 'Eight o'clock,' Harry informed her. The Queen said she had a dinner party to attend that night. Not to be deterred, Harry persisted. 'Will you be cheering England on?' he asked. 'Well, I think one

The Omagh Bomb, 16 August 1998

So many lives lost, so many lives shattered. People have been brought to their knees. Omagh, the once proud county town of Tyrone, is tonight a tragic place.

This afternoon they took away children's clothing, their toys and the pushchairs their mothers had used to bring them here - oblivious of what awaited them.

Boys and girls and women make up the majority of those injured and the majority of those murdered.

Today while the clear-up and search operation continued in absolute silence, the thoughts of ordinary people have been with the victims, not the perpetrators. This is a close-knit town and those who could so easily have been in the wrong place but were not, all know somebody who was.

The car bomb exploded in the midst of hundreds of people. Many of those caught up in this nightmare had been moved from the other end of town. In accordance with the bomb warning, the area around the courthouse had been evacuated. But that warning was bogus and it precipitated wholesale slaughter.

Today the people have been attending church services, they have been praying for those who have been lost and for those who have been injured. And for the future of their town.

John Irvine, ITN, Omagh.

Distressing scenes as rioting marred various World Cup matches in France.

should,' said the Queen. 'They're going to have a very difficult job, I think.' How right she was.

The first real sign that *News at Ten*'s days could be numbered came in September. ITV wanted to change its weekday evening schedule to counteract a small but gradual fall in the number of ITV's viewers. *News at Ten* occupied a space that ITV believed would be better filled by dramas and films. It had asked the Independent Television Commission, which regulates ITV, for permission to move ITN's flagship programme to the earlier time of 6.30pm and have a later news programme from ITN at 11.00pm. That would also mean the end of ITN's early evening news. In November the ITC gave its permission for the move.

During much of the year, Iraq's President Saddam Hussein had tested the patience of America and Britain with his refusal to let United Nations weapons inspectors do their job properly. In December he refused once too often. Just over twelve hours after the inspectors packed up and left, American Cruise missiles were flying over and into Iraq from warships in the Gulf.

It was the night of the newsroom producers' Christmas party. Those who were working on *News at Ten* that night never made it to the party. Most of those at the party left just after ten when the missile attack began. Just before *News at Ten* went on air, it was clear from Baghdad that an American strike was starting. John Suchet, who was presenting the programme, read a short newsflash to say as much. There was then supposed to be a party political broadcast but because of the momentous events of the night that was cancelled at the last minute. *News at Ten* had to get back on the air five minutes faster than they were expecting. The extended programme that followed was compulsive viewing. At that time of night, as people go to bed, the number of people watching *News at Ten* rarely increases. That night it did – from over eight million to more than nine – as confirmation

Lawrence McGinty was dwarfed by Chris Greener –who is seven feet six inches tall – during a report on a conference of the world's tallest people.

came from Prime Minister Tony Blair that the strike had begun.

In the United States, critics of President Clinton accused him of timing the raids to coincide with the impeachment hearings against him. He was accused of lying in evidence he gave about his affair with Monica Lewinsky. The final editions of *News at Ten* this year were dominated by two major international stories running almost in parallel, with a beleaguered president at the centre of both.

And Finally...

On 8 January a pair of Tamworth pigs, later christened Butch and Sundance, carried out a daring escape from a Wiltshire abattoir by going under a fence, evading the slaughterhouse workers, dashing across open ground and diving into the River Avon. When Eric MacInnes carried out his first report on 14 January, the pair had avoided capture for six days.

By the 15th, Butch had been recaptured and the Great Escape came to its inevitable end when Sundance was tracked down and shot with a dart gun. After being checked over by a local vet, the pig was found to be fit and well. Their owner, Arnoldo Dijulio, said the pigs would not be sent to the abattoir and they ended up in an animal sanctuary safe from the butcher's knife.

The Future

NEWS *AT TEN* STARTED AS an experiment in 1967, but it went on to become one of the success stories of British television.

Along the way, the programme radically changed the way in which television news operated, and how it was perceived by the British public. It introduced techniques of presentation, production and journalism that are now regarded as standard. It carved out a worldwide reputation for high quality reporting of news events. It established itself as a programme that made strenuous efforts to make the news of the day interesting and relevant.

The programme was at its best when it hit the big story hard – deploying crews and reporters to the four corners of the earth, securing the crucial pictures, chasing the important interviews, and explaining what was happening in clear and vivid language. Above all, though, it was a programme which cared about its viewers. From the very beginning, it set out to keep firmly in touch with the concerns and priorities of its audience. As a newspaper once neatly put it, '*News at Ten* has its finger on the pulse of the nation.' What is particularly encouraging is that *News at Ten* continued to be a strong programme right up until the end.

But this is no 'And Finally' story. *News at Ten* will come off air on a Friday evening and then, the following Monday at 6.30pm, the same team will

Trevor McDonald and his *News at Ten* production team will be working on the new 6.30pm flagship programme, *The Evening News*.

produce the first edition of ITN's new flagship programme, *The Evening News*.

Many of *News at Ten*'s most recognizable features will be transferred to the new flagship. ITN's well-known and trusted team of reporters will work on the programme. The famous headline 'bongs' of Big Ben will still be there, as will the equally famous 'And Finally' slot. The title music will stay too, but in a new arrangement. The programme will also follow the *News at Ten* editorial approach. It will give high priority to reporting the day's important political and international news events, but at the same time it will also make room for the day's human interest

stories, for consumer and medical items, for media and arts developments, and for sports news.

Nigel Dacre, who's been the editor of *News at Ten* for the past four years and who's in charge of the new programme, sums it up like this: 'It's this broad-based approach to the news which is so important. The BBC tends to be more tightly focused on political and diplomatic developments. We'll cover those developments, but we'll cover so much else besides.'

There will, of course, be new elements on the programme. There will be a new set, a new titles sequence, and a new graphics style. There will be a new emphasis on explaining the issues behind the day's headlines. The running orders will be more flexible and more reactive. And there will be

Nigel Dacre, editor of ITN news on ITV, and Trevor McDonald with the model of the set for the new programme.

more live reports. The other major change is that the programme's production team will go over to using the latest digital technology around the middle of 1999. This includes digital desktop editing and a new computer newsroom system.

The launch of *The Evening News* programme is an exciting opportunity to create a new brand name in British television news. Back in 1967, Alastair Burnet urged people to develop 'a new viewing habit'. And they did – in their millions. Now everyone at ITN is determined to make the new 6.30pm programme as successful as its predecessor, so the audience will do the same again when *The Evening News* begins.

Index

Numbers in *italic* refer to illustrations

Bibliography

Geoffrey Cox, *See It Happen –
The Making of ITN* (Bodley
Head, London, 1983)

Sandy Gall, *News from the Front*
(Heinemann, London, 1994)

Sandy Gall, *Don't Worry About
the Money Now* (Hamish
Hamilton, London, 1983)

Michael Nicholson, *A Measure of
Danger* (HarperCollins, London,
1991).

Jeremy Potter (ed.), *The Official
History of the IBA – The ITV
Companies*

Chronicle of the 20th Century
(Dorling Kindersley, London,
1995)